GVA
A Universe of Creativity

Introduction by **Mario Pisani**

l'ARCAEDIZIONI

Photographic Credits

Carlos Escobar
pages 14, 18, 26, 27, 36, 54, 55, 56 (top), 92, 93 (top), 95, 104

Scott Mc Donald, Hedrich-Blessing
pages 16, 17, 19, 20, 21, 22, 24, 25, 28, 29, 30, 31, 32, 33, 38,
39, 40 (top), 50, 53, 56 (below), 57, 58, 59, 60, 61, 92 (below), 94

Alejandro López
Tapalpa Country Club

Jesus Cervantes
La Vista Country Club

Chief Editor of Collection
Maurizio Vitta

Publishing Coordinator
Franca Rottola

Editorial Staff
Cristina Rota

Graphic Design
l'Arca Edizioni spa

Editing
Martyn J. Anderson

Colour-separation
LitofilmsItalia, Bergamo

Printing
Bolis Poligrafiche SpA, Azzano San Paolo (BG)

First published January 2003

ISBN 88-7838-120-9

Contents

WITHDRAWN

Preface

by *Jose Manuel and Jaime Gomez Vazquez Aldana*

With the beginning of this century, Man has begun to show respect for his own planet. He is now more aware of the need to protect his surroundings and conserve nature.

Gomez Vazquez Aldana and Associates shares these thoughts. Therefore, through careful planning, creativity and excellence in designs and execution, it has been able to produce the dynamic circumstances needed for achieving a complete success in the areas of aesthetics, usefulness, economics and spirituality, resulting in nature being left intact and the initial investment increasing over the years.

This philosophy has convinced us to come up with adequate responses to the ever more complex problems of urban development and architecture of our times.

This is how we set out to recover the human habitat, integrating it into a context of dignity, order and beauty, essential elements for the perfect performance of human activities in clear harmony with human surroundings, nature and the cosmos.

We believe in team work. Ever since 1961 when we began our activities as a group, we have put together a large group of professionals over the years. Based on our experience, research and constant searching, we provide proper solutions to the dynamic conditions of human habitat. From the beginning we have designed and created structures that not only serve their purpose but are also a delight for our eyes and spirit and are in perfect harmony with the surroundings.

Today our world-class team of over 150 professionals has become one of the most prestigious firms specializing in architecture and regional and urban planning.

Specific dimensions exist. There are topographical limits, ecosystems and available services that have to share their function with business and finance. The ability we have to combine these factors is a coherent and successful achievement, enabling us to provide clients with outstanding facilities which are successful not only for the users of the projects but also for investors.

With the idea of increasing our territorial coverage and broadening the horizons of our activities, we formed a strategic alliance with Peridian International, one of the most prestigious landscape architectural firms, with whom we have worked jointly on a large variety of projects throughout Mexico and Latin America.

Our professional practice has resulted in the creation of a well-coordinated team covering all aspects of design and engineering; Arquitectura de Interiores and Peridian are Group companies involved in interior designs and landscape architecture respectively.

The accomplishment of our goals is based on the development and self-realization of the human and professional qualities of each member of our team. We believe in community service by providing our clients with a better service. In pursuit of these goals and as a steadfast premise, our works must be functional, technological, economic, social, aesthetic and environmental successes and, first and foremost, human achievements. We think and believe that, as architects, we must assume the role of coordinators and catalyst of the essential contributions of all other experts and consultants because the best solutions to real needs are accomplished through an integral project.

All quality professional work must have its just rewards. We believe that our clients are the most important part of our firm and should participate with the work team in order to reach a full definition of the final solution of each project.

The Group is currently developing several projects throughout the country and abroad, ranging from hotels and apartment buildings to shopping malls, movie theaters and private residences. In each and every one, excellence in design is combined with financial logic and excellent client service, the principles of quality that drive each and every one of our projects.

Vitality and Tranquillity

by *Mario Pisani*

"Architecture is not an art, it is a natural function. It is born from the earth, like animals and plants".
Fernand Léger

"We have had enough of fashion designers, models, trends and revivals. Of cultural movements, modern-day illnesses, compulsory thinking, and what is "in" and what is "out". Of opinion leaders, punk reincarnations of Lord Brummell, neo-dandies that boast about being alive. Of new books on etiquette, the latest lists of places to go on holiday, mass idolatry, "plastic" singers, restaurants that you have to eat at, and epoch-making exhibitions. Of marks, stars and asterisks for films, books and food, lists of best-sellers, opinion polls, and magazine covers. We have had enough of all the false novelties, false information, pictures and surfaces praised for their lack of substance (...) We have had enough of fashion".
Ugo Volli, *Rifiuto del Conformismo*

Glancing through pictures of the works of architecture designed by the GVA Gomez Vazquez Aldana & Associates firm, the first thing to catch the eye, even just after a quick, rapid analysis carried out rather superficially and in great haste, is the way they fit in with Ugo Volli's thinking or, in other words, a powerful and clearly evident rejection of the kind of all-embracing conformism, which is our modern-day multi-media society.

This can be seen from the Los Tules Residential Development and Fiesta Americana in Puerto Vallarta, a huge and elaborate holiday complex designed way back in the 1970s and still resounding with the echo of an economic boom of an opulent society nonchalantly addressing energy and pollution issues, although in certain details you can already hear the rolling thunder of the crisis in the International Style leading to first the crumbling and then total collapse of its empire of signs.

This is even more evident in the Marriott Casamagna Cancun Resort in Cancun, completed in the late 1990s, a period when the Postmodern style still reigned supreme through its revival in architectural syntagms borrowed from European building tradition and history or, even more specifically, from the Mediterranean basin, as in this case with its pergola, loggia and portico, as well as the enclosed square and spacious inside hall, a sort of magical Aladdin's den. Similar remarks apply to Mayan Palace in Guadalajara, where alongside the distant memory of the American firm Arcquitectonica's idiom (developed under the guidance of Bernardo Fort-Brescia and Laurinda Hope Spear) we also find a sculptural concatenation of unusual combinations of tight, compact structures, or to Parque Milenium in the city of Puebla, designed like a sort of entrance gate to the very heart of the city from the urban suburbs.

GVA's architecture quietly talks to us of a silent rejection of trendy linguistic conformism, such as Minimalism, High Tech, the sculptural emphasis of Frank Gehry's works and, most particularly, Deconstructivism, architecture that appears to have been mutated by the thrill of collapse and ecstasy of disaster.

What it does have to offer is its careful stylistic attention to the purposes for which a building is designed, which, in most cases, means serving the high and priceless calling of hospitality; a desire to make those familiar wealthy tourists at home when they arrive in Mexico with their heads full of the usual clichés originating from Hollywood films. This architecture is also particularly attentive to how a building fits into its site location, simultaneously respecting and taking full advantage of all its incredible possibilities and extraordinary stylistic potential.

In GVA's works, construction really does seem capable of taking on shape and form, as in its most emblematic and convincing examples – I am referring to the Robinson Club in Tulun (1993), Tapalpa Country Club in Tapalpa (1994) and La Vista Country Club in Puebla (1997) – drawing on all the setting's eloquent potential in that very special combination of sea, sun, and luxuriant parks and gardens – almost a tamed jungle – in which the buildings are cleverly inserted.
All this is not just found in his first constructions, it is also most definitely present in his modern-day designs built in a media-dominated society in which the Star System has even exploded into the world of architecture, a period in which news of flashy new events fill the pages of our newspapers only to be immediately forgotten the next day, a sort of nothing created from the transient effects of pictures that only exist in the architect's mind, having no roots and hence all set to vanish and dissolve like snow in the sunshine.

Looking at the results of recent competitions – both major competitions in which the aforementioned stars are invited to take part and also more recent constructions erected in all kinds of capital cities right across the world respecting the blandest of contemporary building standards – we, too, cannot help wanting to shout out that "we have had enough of fashion". This rebellion is, in certain respects, the very structural frame on which this firm has built up its vast experience, working mainly (though not only) in Mexico on designs like huge hotel complexes, in which we find the same old sign (or so we would like to think, seeing how witty it is), as in a big hotel in Miami: "If you can't sleep, before you blame our beds or pillows, examine your own conscience". Architecture lending careful attention to natural light, the splendour of colours, local stylistic traditions and interaction with nature as one of the most intriguing features of Mexican buildings. Even back before Columbus discovered America, Mexico had an extremely advanced culture whose main characteristics, connected with a sense of place and deeply entrenched in local taste, emerge all the time, entering into fervid dialectical relations with its new constructions ever since the first new buildings appeared on the urban scene right after the Spanish conquest and right down to the works of an extraordinary person like Luis Barragàn, who achieved a happy synthesis between European experimentation (focusing on Mediterranean gardens with their distinctly Arabian connotations) and local styles.

In a recent presentation Alessandro Anselmi wrote that "architecture is always hovered ambiguously between knitting in with the natural surroundings and sublimation in conceptual space, generating that sense of 'wonder', as Alberti put it, without which everything deteriorates into mere building. In order to effectively come to terms with this tricky transition from tectonics to architecture, every period in history and semantic realm has worked out its own complicated theories and, even more significantly, intricate operations touching on every category involved in the design and constructions of an architectural event; in other words, architecture has always striven to genuinely symbolise historically determined anthropologic contents".

This quote gets right to the heart of contemporary debate: how to fit into the natural context, the presence and exalting of what is already there, what

the Latins called the ability to be in harmony with the genius loci, respecting its desires and grasping on-site the smooth narrative it relates, ready to be exalted and sublimed in conceptual space which, in Greek architecture, produced for instance the Erechtheum or that marvel known as the House of Winds, again in Athens. GVA's major territorial projects are fine examples in this respect, notably those in Marina Ixtapa, Ixtapa Zihuatanejo or Marina Guaymas, in which the layout of functional spaces and action taken on the precious natural environment have always be handled taking the utmost care over the balance between architecture and nature.

Another interesting point is the proper awareness that architecture has always aimed to – and we need only take the new St. Peter's in the Vatican in Rome or, more recently, the Great Library of France designed by Dominique Perrault in Paris – transform historically determined anthropologic contents into a symbol.

In my opinion, this design firm works along these very lines, knitting in with the environment and exalting its potential connotations in a magical combination of light, colour, landscape and materials used. The firm's architecture also seem to be acutely aware of the needs of people using what seem to be golden havens. All these tourist villages transmit a sense of comfort connected with happy outdoor holidays in close contact with the sun and sea, rather than just focusing on image for image's sake, often inevitably resulting in close relations with the fashion system.
These are also the lines along which I have attempted to make a critical analysis of the works designed and built by this internationally well-known Mexican architectural and planning firm.

Holiday Resorts

"Leisure time, currently all the rage, is actually just a short break between two mechanically predetermined periods of work , holidays booked in advance at a certain time of year, mass holidays, again justified in terms of production that encourages consumption, important evidence of the rationally organised nature of a society that has come to think of and actually bring about the artificial creation of the spontaneous".
Franco Ferrarotti,
Produzione e tempo libero

There can be no doubt that travelling, or better still holidays seen as an experience, no longer really exist. A ghost that has vanished and now belongs to other periods in history when travelling was a learning experience in quest of knowledge, just like back in the days of the grand tours of Italy.

Nowadays, holidays might be described as a fast way of taking a large number of people from one part of the world to another, usually by plane, everything geared to speed and efficiency. The best way to fit in with the workings of the holiday industry is to get people to their destinations as quickly as possible: a holiday club or tourist village, where everything is laid on and you only need make the odd trip to see the surroundings and how the locals live. Just like cruises, you only stay for about a week before going back to the same old boring routine, rejuvenated and with a good tan and, of course, a few extra pounds and photos and souvenirs to prove you had been to these exotic places.

Nobody can say what Franz Kafka wrote in one of his short, surreal dialogues:

"Where are you going, sir"? "I do not know", I replied, "just away from here, that is the only way I can get to my destination". "So you know where you are going?", he pointed out. "Yes", I replied, "I've told you. Out of here, that's my goal". "Have you any supplies with you"?, he said [...] "I do not need any, – I replied – the journey is so long, I'll starve to death unless I find something along the way. No supplies will save me. Fortunately, it is an extraordinary journey".

Our architectural designers are quite familiar with the system around which elite holidays are organised, designed for the upper-middle bracket of opulent society, and they take it well into account when they put their hands to designing a new tourist village, of course each with its own special features and characteristics and, most importantly, in incredible places exalting nature's unique combination of sea and sky. For example, the Robinson Club in Tulum commissioned by an important European tour operator specialising in All Inclusive Hotels, which was completed in 1993, is not far from an interesting archeological site full of relics of Mayan culture. Its architecture is inspired by local buildings constructed between the late-19th century and early-20th century when Europe was under the dominion of the Liberty style.

Under the client's careful scrutiny, a subtle game of allusions and interaction breaks out between them and tourists, a careful staging of happy holidays where everything is possible and helped along by spaces designed for congregating and socialising, encouraging chance meetings with the aid of the sunshine and sea, well aware that, to quote Jorge Luis Borges, "El mar es un antiguo lenguaje que yo no alcanzo a decifrar" (The sea is an ancient language I cannot decipher).

The architecture here is not supposed to surprise or astonish but speak in high, dulcet tones. And to this end, tradition teaches us that it is not preservation and conservation but the ability to make changes and alterations that counts, as with the Fiesta Americana Merida in Merida in the Yucatan (1994) or La Vista Country Club in Puebla (1997) – i.e. belonging to contexts – responding to changing needs and ideas of the world.

It is worth remembering that history does not teach conservation in architectural design but presents a long series of innovations. Tradition is the sedimentation and gradual stratification of innovations interacting, often in conflict due to the speed with which they weave together and also because, as Italo Calvino points out in the American Lessons, "transience, diversity, instability, rapidity" are the key values of contemporary society, the values we must measure up to.

Conclusions

"Even prose has its beauty; going neither one way nor the other, trying to look both right an left. But is this always possible? Or even desirable? These conflicting passions are the flame feeding history, the history we are told about and that we, in turn, try to understand. How could you not suffer or not get excited along the way, even though it is a crime against the sacred rules of impartiality"?
Fernand Braudel

The firm's latest works, like Isla Dorada, a self contained resort community (1999), located between Bojorquez and Nichupte lagoons, a group of small islands connected by quiet channels for sailing along, where there are twelve complexes of houses, villas, hotels and shopping malls, like Secret Punta Cana (2001) in the Dominican Republic with a 367-room five-star hotel with 34 suites and five different restaurants, a gym, children's club, theatre, a number of shops and other attractions or the project for the Martyrs' Sanctuary in Guadalajara planned to be completed in 2004, have a number of other features in common worth mentioning.

It also seems that the art of constructing meaningful buildings and landmarks for the cultural debate of the age in which we live, slotted into unforgettable settings, needs to soften down the confrontation and turn itself into a sort of art of modelling in tune with the environment. Here again, as in the case of sculpture in certain respects, in addition to the ability to set about and complete a major composition, we can also sense a certain global vision in the shaping of spaces and, above all, in their relation to the landscape and the patient work of an artisan working away on the interiors, taking care of all the details and minor features to complete the work in craftsmanlike fashion. Even in the age of computer technology and the Internet, hand finishing is the clearest evidence of the firm's craftsmanship.

After all, we know that people caress things whose form attracts their attention. Personal contact makes even a simple form extraordinary and magnificent. Hands explore, almost without being aware of it, as if to reveal and exalt an existing form. Even perfect architecture needs hands to transmit a certain impulse and warmth, to disclose certain subtle features lost to the eye, and it takes hands to bring out its overall softness and gentleness.

Stone, wood, brick and all natural materials used so cleverly and exposed to atmospheric agents record, in an instantaneous and simultaneous spatial form on their concrete profiles, not just the bitter transition from day to night, the skies as they open and heat up or the rain, blowing wind or heat of the sunshine, but even the vitality resulting from every single contact they receive. I think the sincerest characteristic of GVA's architecture is what you sense upon closer and more meticulous examination, mainly by studying the site plans, design sketches and sections, as well as the general rejection of fashion.

In relation to what has just been said, the following comments by Kenneth Frampton in Tectonics and Architecture sums all this up better than I can: "In the end, everything depends as much on how exactly it was carried out as on any open manifestation of its form. This is not to deny spatial ingenuity, but merely to exalt it through the way it is carried out. This means that the way a work is presented is inseparable from its foundations and the authority with which its structure interacts in its connections, joints and articulations, the pattern of its cladding and the shape of its windows. Located at the junction of culture and nature, building just as much involves the ground as built form. Just like farming, its task is to alter the surface of the ground so as to take care of it, in accordance with Heidegger's concept of Gelassenheit or tranquillity. This explains the idea of 'building a place', as Mario Botta put it so memorably, which is more important than just creating isolated objects and, in this respect, building involves topos just as much as technique. Moreover, despite the privatising of modern society, architecture (due to the way it is opposed to building) tends to promote space designed for the public in contrast with the privacy of a Domus. At the same time, it just as much involves creation of a place and passage of time as space and form. Light, water, wind, and the action of atmosphere agents, are all responsible for consuming it. In the sense that its continuity transcends mortality,

building forms the foundations of life and culture. In this respect, it is neither high art nor high technology. In as much as it challenges time, it is by definition anachronistic. GVA has developed their work based on the Jose Manuel approach :"Architecture is a harmony of structural elements, delimiting space that produces poetry and beauty where the spirit reigns". Durability and curability are its grounding features. In the end, it has nothing to do with immediacy, while it has plenty to do with the ineffable. What was it that Barragan said? "Any work of architecture that fails to express calmness, fails in its spiritual mission. The task of the age in which we live is to combine vitality and tranquillity".

I could not agree more. The idea of calmness, in a combination of vitality and tranquillity, is also what inspires the work of Gomez Vazquez Aldana and Associates.

Works

Los Tules Residential Development and Fiesta Americana

Puerto Vallarta

Completion date
1979

Owner
Cia Hotelera de Vallarta s.a.

Architect
GVA & Associates

The Los Tules Residential Development and Fiesta Americana Puerto Vallarta tourist and residential development was built over 11 hectares in front of Banderas Bay. 2.5 hectares were used for the hotel and 8.5 for residential development. The property is oblong with about 550 meters of beach front, bounded on the south by Los Tules estuary.

The hotel is located in the northernmost part of the development to give it privacy from the rest of the area dedicated to the residential estate. This latter area was designed with 5 clusters of apartments and villas, each cluster surrounding plazas where the different swimming pools are located. These clusters are concentrated in the area nearest the beach to respect the existing palm groves at the rear of the property. Somewhat like a vein, an extension of Los Tules estuary enters the property to give the project its own special attraction.

The cluster layout allowed development to take place in stages, which was a determining factor in the economic financial strategy for carrying out the project. The residential area holds 300 apartments with 1, 2 or 3 bedrooms and studio villas, all with hotel services.

The cluster development also allowed different sales options such as full-time ownership, divided ownership and time-sharing, with all units holding onto their privacy.

The four level apartment buildings have a staggered front, somewhat like terraces, for all apartments at all levels.

The 45,000-square-meter residential area has large palm-covered garden areas as well as 6 tennis courts open to all residents.

The Grand Tourism Class Fiesta Americana Puerto Vallarta Hotel has 300 rooms located in a 9-level horseshoe-shaped building opening onto the beach. The public areas located on the ground floor of the main building are the lobby bar, a specialty restaurant, the entertainment lounge and the convention areas. The main lobby and reception areas are in a large building covered by a 30-meter-diameter thatched roof which is 20 meters high.

This space is initially striking for its distinctly tropical flavor and spaciousness, which together with local materials offer visitors a glimpse of regional architecture.

The restaurant-cafeteria, located near the beach in the pool area, is also covered with a thatched roof.

The public areas also include a discotheque open to people from outside the complex. The hotel has 25,000 sq.m of construction.

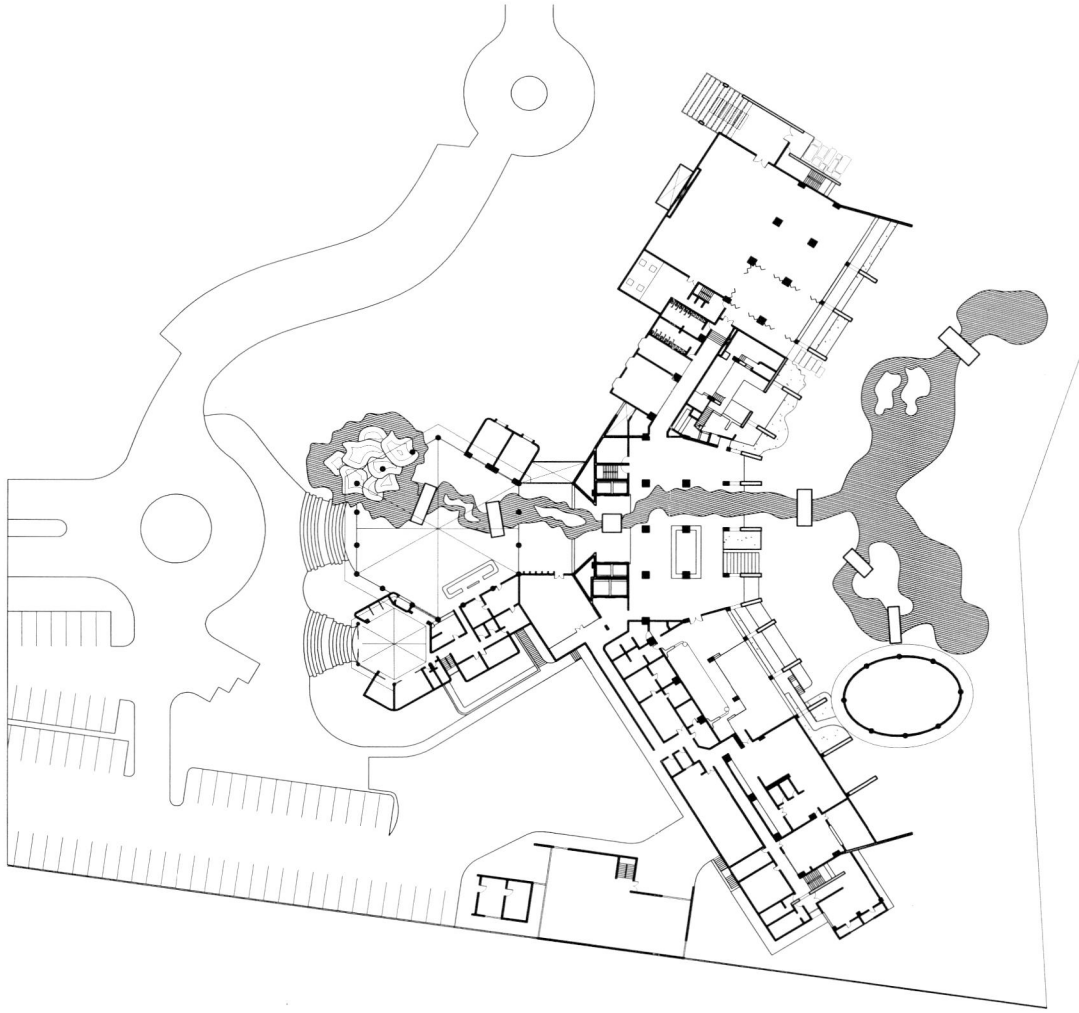

Ground floor plan.

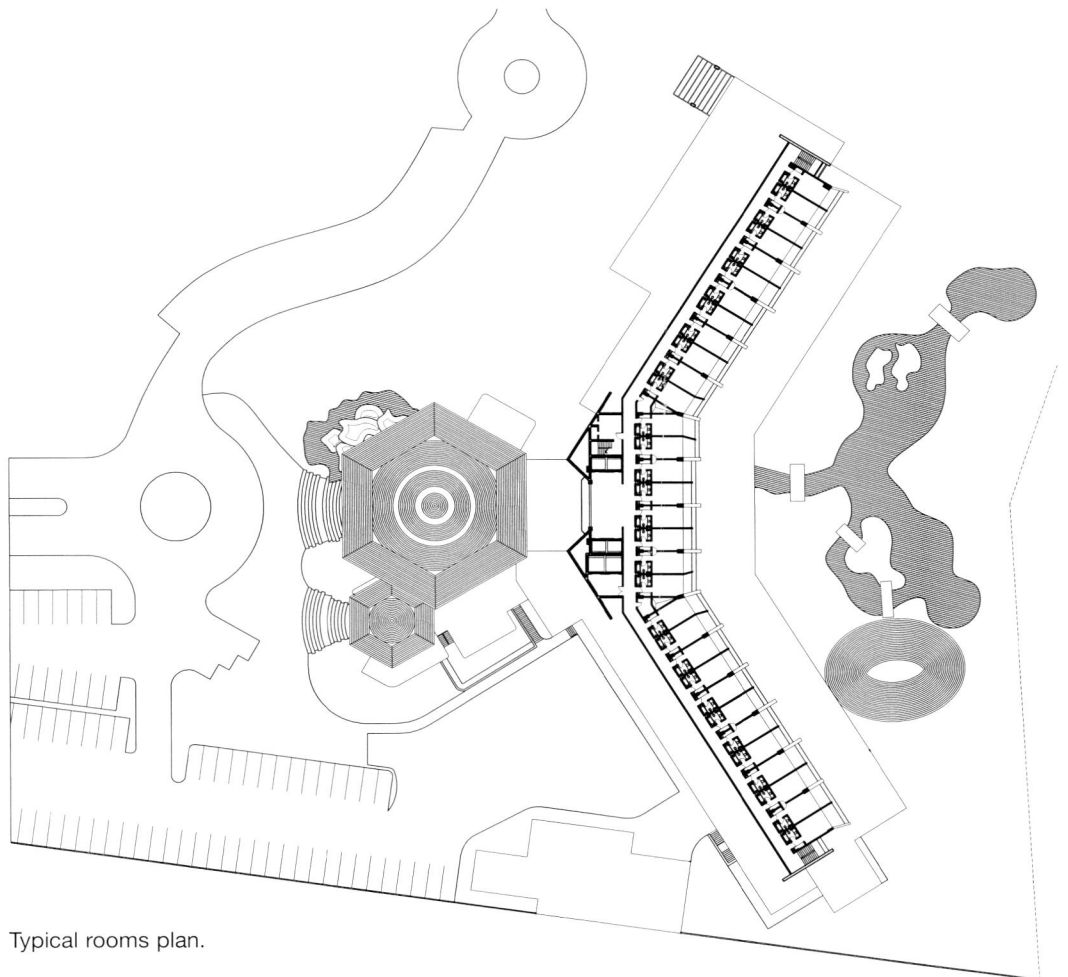

Typical rooms plan.

Opposite page, aerial view of the hotel.
Next page, panoramic view by night of the complex with Puerto Vallarta in the background.

Above, views of the residential
indoors.
Opposite page, view of the main
entrance.

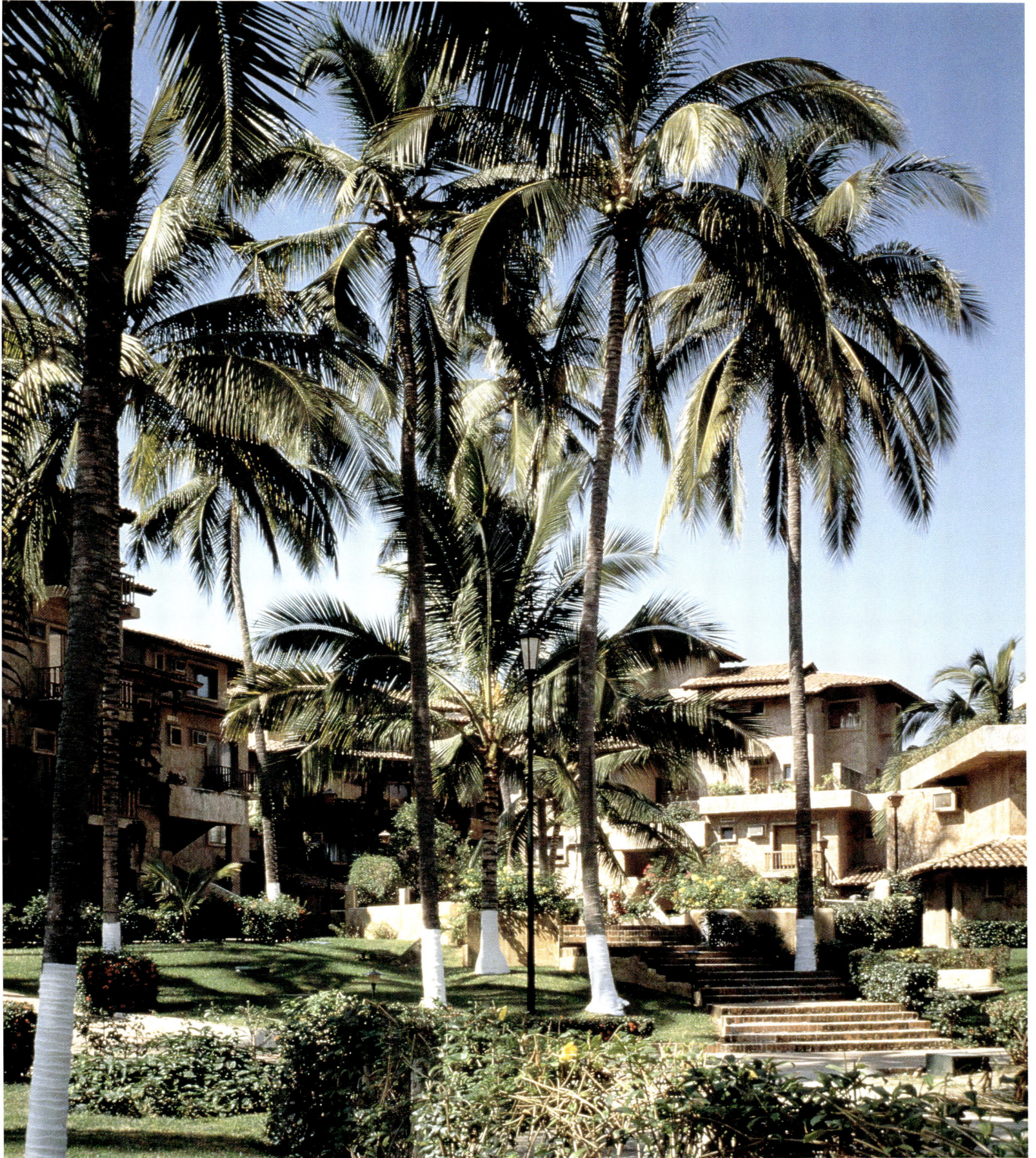

Opposite page, view of the spacious hall.
Above, view of the complex from the garden.

Marriott Casamagna Cancun Resort

Cancun

Completion date
October, 1990

Owner
Grupo Cemex

Architect
GVA & Associates

Interior design
Arquitectura de Interiores

Engineering
GVA & Associates

The Marriott Casamagna Cancun Hotel is located in the Cancun hotel zone on about a 35,000-square-meter piece of property with 200 meters of beach front. It is Grand Tourism category resort hotel with 450 rooms and world class convention facilities.

The architecture of the hotel is a syncretic combination of Mediterranean architecture with the tropical hotel concept: arcades, hanging gardens and arbors, all integrated seamlessly into the outdoor areas. It was inspired by Mediterranean gardens with large reflecting pools to underscore the symmetry of the gardens. There is also a classic-shaped swimming pool surrounded by a semicircular colonnade that accentuates the view of the beautiful Caribbean Ocean.

The project includes a horseshoe-shaped main building with the central part facing the beach and the side wings perpendicular to the beach. It has four stories plus a basement to house hotel services.

The two-story-high ground floor of this building holds the front desk, lobby, lobby lounge, shop area and business offices. Four levels of rooms above this area give shape to the atrium that runs the length of the building, giving a sense of interior spaciousness.

The side wings holding the rest of the rooms and hotel suites are six levels tall and also form an atrium that runs the length of the building, with an open two-level-high arcade in the lower part that integrates the outside areas, offering spaciousness and fluidity.

There are four elements independent from the main building that house the casual restaurant, the poolside restaurant and bar, the games room and the specialty restaurant.

Convention center facilities include a large ballroom with room for 800 people that can be divided into 8 rooms, as well as 3 meeting rooms and a board room.

Above, the symmetry of the indoor gardens was inspired by Mediterranean gardens.

Opposite page, panoramic view of the swimming pool surrounded by semicircular colonnade.

Next pages, aerial view of the horseshoe-shaped main building in front of the Caribbean Ocean.

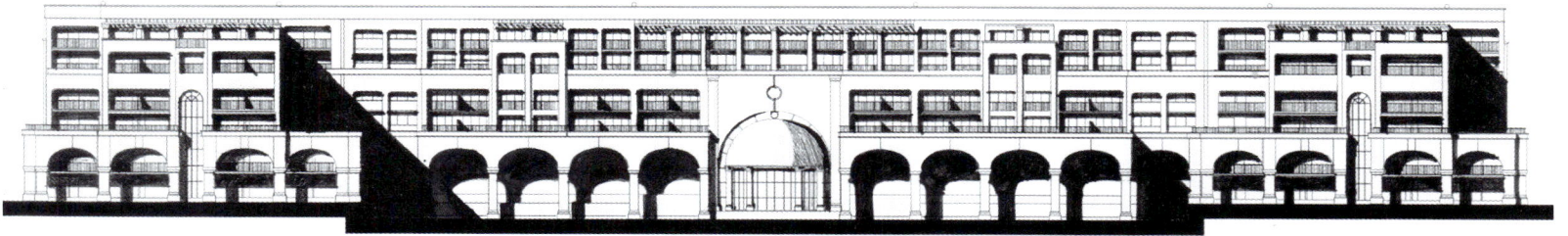

Main elevation.

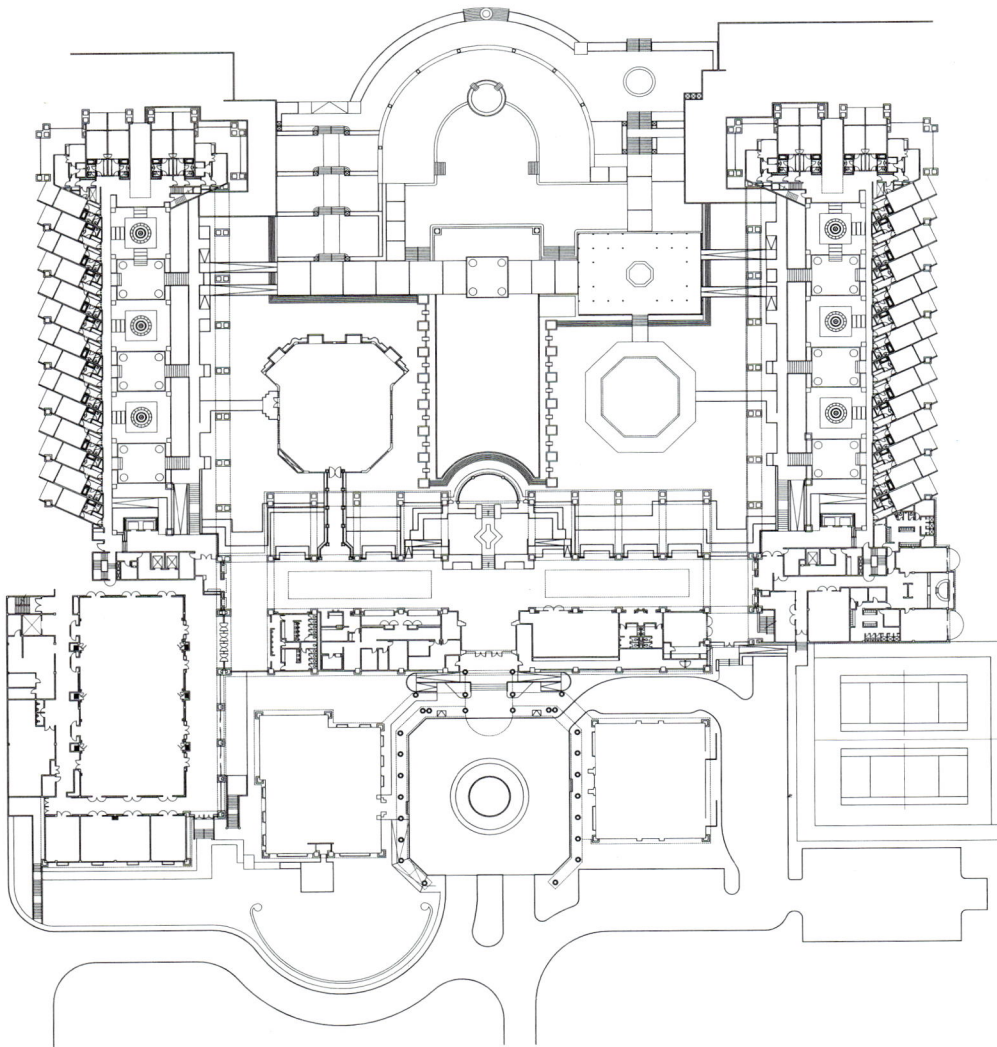

Main floor plan.

Above, view of the motor lobby.
Opposite page, view of the pool from
the colonnade.

Views of the atrium that runs the length of the building with an open two-level-high arcade in the lower part.

Opposite page, view of the main atrium. Above, view of the specialty restaurant.

Left, view of one of the wings holding the rooms.

FIESTA AMERICANA
CORAL BEACH.

Fiesta Americana Coral Beach Hotel

Cancun

Completion date
December, 1990

Owner
Promotora Caribe Cancun

Architect
GVA & Associates

Landscape
Peridian de Mexico

Interior Design
Arquitectura de Interiores

This special category hotel, located in the Cancun, Quintana Roo tourist zone on a 34,600 sq.m piece of property facing Caracol Beach and Mujeres Bay at Punta Cancun, has a constructed surface area of 100,000 sq.m and houses 602 suites.

The main design premise was to have each of the rooms facing the sea by taking advantage of the elongated property. The project layout placed the motor lobby in the middle, a sort of hub from which the two main bodies of rooms spread out on levels 8 and 9 respectively, with 7 elevators for guests and 4 serving service purposes.

The 5-story-high main lobby is situated in the middle of the hotel, an important space surrounded by plants and sitting rooms, all of which follow the design and are integrated into the lobby bar with a beautiful ocean view from the entrance. This space distributes toward the east and west towers of the project.

The east tower houses "Coral Ref.", a gourmet restaurant that seats 100 diners, and the "Café Viña del Mar" cafeteria that seats up to 280 people. The convention area is also in this tower and consists of three levels of meeting rooms, business centers and the main hall with an overall capacity of 2,500 people, 1,200 people in an auditorium facility and 1,000 for banquettes.

The spa boutique on the third floor of the tower has an ocean view and hydro massage tubs, sauna, steam baths, barber shop and so forth. The hotel also has a specialty restaurant, "La Joya", that offers its services for up to 220 people, both guests and visitors.

The group lobby is in the west tower, a small area with service facilities both inside and outside the hotel. The business offices are also located here as well as an important tennis club with three indoor courts and all the relevant facilities, such as a Pro shop, stands, restrooms, energy snack bar, and so on.
Hotel services are located in the basement and distributed throughout the development, strategically located to meet the project requirements.

The outside areas are extremely spacious given the features of the property, with a 200-meter-long swimming pool integrated into the "Isla Contoy" restaurant seating 120 guests, as well as the snack bar, the "Sunrise and Bikini Bar" and the "Sunset Bar" that serve the beach. Each tower has 480 standard suites, 80 master suites and 2 presidential suites. Each standard suite has a surface area of 48 sq.m including a living room with an ocean view, and a bathroom with a sink, toilet and bath tub.

Schematic section.

Opposite page, aerial view of the
hotel facing Coral Beach and
Mujeres Bay.

Above, view of the motor lobby
which has been placed in the
middle of the complex.

Next page, panoramic view of the
pool which is integrated into the
restaurant and snack bar areas.

Views of the motor lobby, a sort of
hub from which the two main bodies
of rooms spread out on eight and
nine levels.

Above, detail of the terrace.
Opposite page, detail of the facade.
The aim was to have each
room facing the sea.

Robinson Club

Tulum

Completion date
1993

Owner
Robinson Club

Architect
GVA & Associates

Landscape design
Peridian de México

The All Inclusive Robinson Club Resort is located very near to what was once one of the major settlements back in Mayan times: Tulum.

This hotel, located on the shores of the Caribbean, stands out from other archeological sites. It is located in Xpu-Ha on the Yucatan Peninsula facing the island of Cozumel on a 300,000-square-meter piece of land with a typical Caribbean beach.

Robinson Club Tulum was developed by the Gomez Vazquez Aldana and Associates Group for one of the most prestigious and important European All Inclusive hotel chains that selected this site to serve anybody visiting this part of Mexico, whether for relaxation purposes or to learn more about Mayan culture and civilization while feeling close to nature, far from any vestige of large, noisy urban sprawl.

The architectural design was integrated into the landscape in an effort not to compete with the serenity of nature, the intense green of the mangroves and the turquoise blue of the sea.

This was an important prevailing factor in making the decision to locate the hotel at a distance of about 80 meters from the sea, so that visitors looking up from the beach would never guess there was a 300-room hotel development, making this hotel a very special attraction.

The project was integrated through the creation of three small islands surrounded by small saltwater ponds. A 100-room building was constructed on each of the islands.

The main building houses public services including three restaurants and all the other services required of a resort hotel.

Visitors arrive at a reception area through a palm grove, so that they feel as if they are entering a place remote from civilization.

The buildings were imaginatively designed to look like Mexican Caribbean architecture from the late-19th and early-20th century, if there had actually been any predecessors on the entire peninsula. It is worth mentioning that this area has been developed to cater for world class tourism in a relatively short space of time; years ago it was practically virgin country.

Robinson Club Tulum has swimming pools, sports areas and a mini-club, all this based on the theme of "Jungle Gardens".

Due to the fact the hotel is so far from other towns, a 100-room building was constructed to house staff working for the hotel.

Robinson Club Tulum is a hotel that has become a real attraction on the international tourist map because it is located on a site brimming with magic, scenery and living nature.

Above, panoramic view of the pool.
Opposite page, view of the channel;
the project was integrated through
the creation of three small islands
surrounded by small saltwater
ponds.

Site plan.

Opposite page, view of the bar.
Above, detail of the facade.

The Ritz Carlton

Cancun

Completion date
April, 1993

Owner
Grupo Escorpion

Architect
**GVA & Associates /
Guillermo Carrillo Arenas**

Engineering
**GVA & Associates /
Guillermo Carrillo Arenas**

Interior design
Arquitectura de Interiores

Landscape design
Peridian de Mexico

This Grand Tourism Hotel opened to business in April of 1993, filling a need to lodge sophisticated local and international tourists visiting the beautiful beaches of the Mexican Caribbean.

The goal upon designing this 372 room hotel, each with an ocean view, was to integrate Mexican construction, tradition and culture with a classic refined European style, and to interpret the Ritz Carlton style in fixtures and ambience with intimacy and good taste, so that guests visiting the hotel may enjoy their vacation or business trip surrounded by culture, sports and romance.

With the above features as well as the formal aspect and quality service, one of the trade magazines awarded it the title of the Premier Hotel in Latin America and it now is ranked 50th in the world.

Nothing is missing at this hotel in terms of guest comfort with its health spa, beauty salon, boutiques, magnificent meeting rooms and convention facilities that offer service and attention to between 8 and 1,050 people in a 1,234-square-meter ballroom.

The main lobby leads through to the lobby lounge offering a great panoramic view of the Caribbean, the beach, two swimming pools and a beach club, all this surrounded by tropical landscaping and fountains.

Properly lit tennis courts are at the front on the roof of the parking structure. The junior suites, 40 executive suites, 3 presidential suites, the lounge club, as well as the art nouveau speciality restaurant, cafeteria, and bar and grill are in the central part of the hotel distributed around an 8 story high atrium.

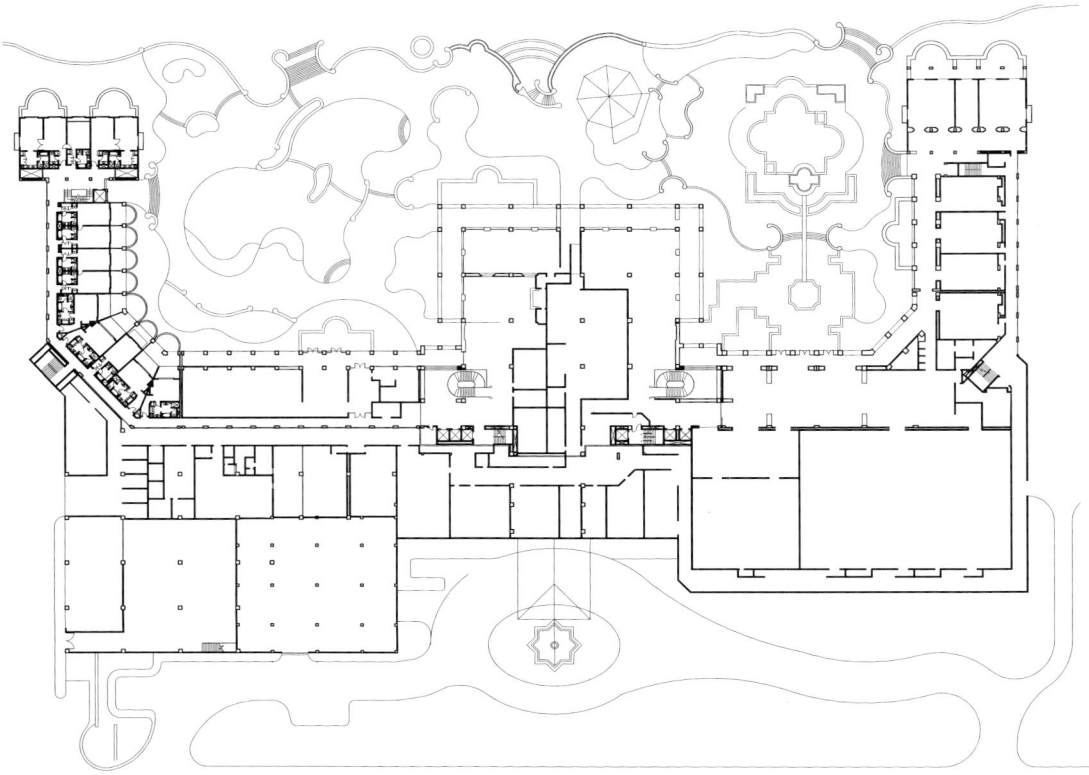

Main floor plan.

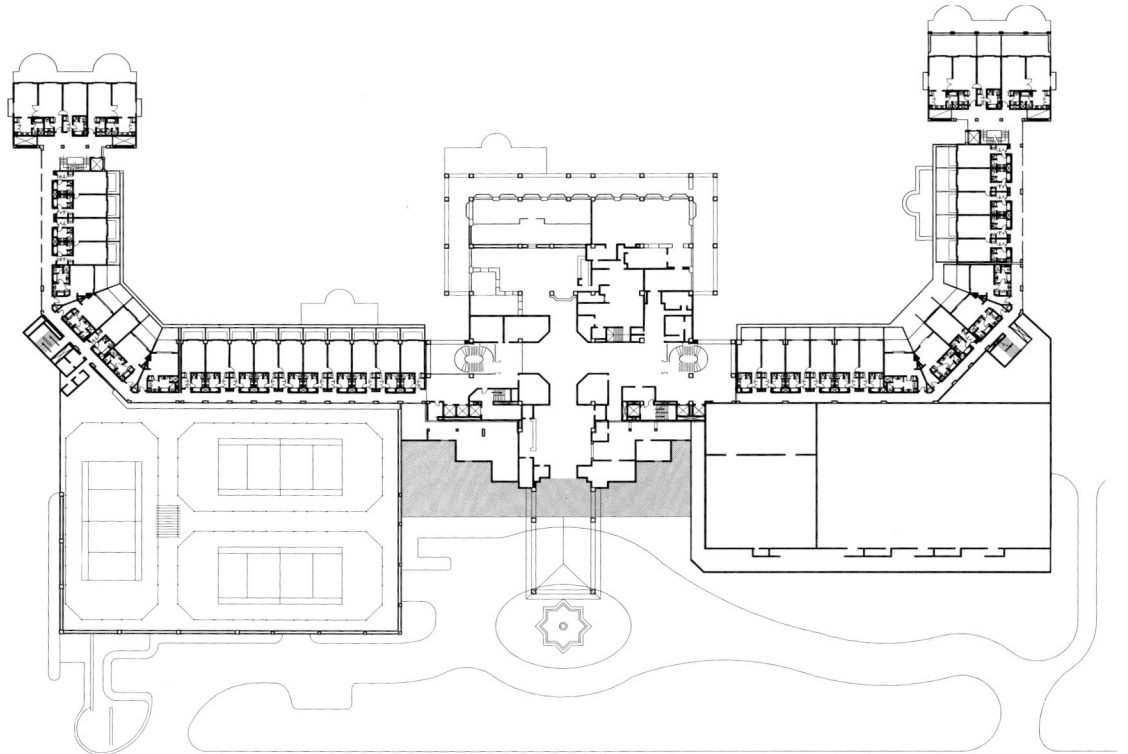

Typical rooms plan.

Opposite page, panoramic view of the pool which is surrounded by tropical landscaping and fountains.

Next pages, aerial view from the Caribbean Ocean; each room has an ocean view.

Top, aerial view of the main facade. Above, panoramic view from the beach.

Opposite page, main building terrace.

Above, view of the main entrance.
Opposite page, one of the main
building terraces.

Top, view of the pool by night.
Above, convention hall corridor.
Opposite page, view of the lobby
lounge which offers a great
panoramic view of the Caribbean.

Tapalpa Country Club

Jalisco

Completion date
1994

Owner
Promotora Tapalpa

Planning, Urban design and Architecture
GVA & Associates

Landscape design
Peridian de México

Interior Design
Arquitectura de Interiores

Engineering
GVA & Associates

Tapalpa, the most popular mountain resort, is situated in a typical little rural town up in Mexico's wooded mountains.

This is where a project was designed to create the first great mountain development with a golf course in Mexico with the basic idea of conserving the beauty of the surrounding environment.

This mountain tourist and residential development has a golf course, a club house and a series of attractions that are normal for this kind of development.

With an unbeatable location on the slopes of the Western Sierra Madre range in the middle of a pine forest, it offers beautiful panoramic views from any spot. The main views are of the Colima volcano, the valley and the reservoir, the roof tops of the picturesque town of Tapalpa, and the golf course itself.

Located just 90 minutes from Guadalajara, Mexico's second largest city, it has a surface area of 183 hectares, which have been planned and designed to house a wide variety of attractions, including a Grand Class horizontal hotel with log cabin style suites, each with their own private terrace, kitchenette, living room, bedroom and fireplace.

The par 36 golf course has a caddies' club, pro shop, snack bar, 4 tennis courts, a clubhouse with both an indoor and outdoor pool, restaurant, bar, aerobics room, and restrooms and dressers for women, men and children.

The log cabins have 2, 3 or 4 bedrooms on 1,500 sq.m lots.

The outdoor area covers about 10,000 sq.m with attractions such as volleyball, archery, hiking, canoeing, rock climbing as well as excursions to the waterfall, the boulders or the pretty town of Tapalpa, whose legacy dates back to when it was founded in the late-19th century.

The design was enhanced thanks to balance, downplaying the architecture to integrate it into the natural landscape, surrounded by all the comforts and amenities of modern life. All the spaces were created and designed according to the basic concept and premise of integrating local material into the form and function of the interior spaces.

Thanks to the goal of maintaining, integrating and respecting harmony with the natural surroundings together with the landscaping design, Tapalpa Country Club has earned the title of "A Window onto Paradise".

And today, everyone can enjoy it.

Opposite page, view of the cabins which have their own private terrace, kitchen, living room, bedroom and fireplace.
Top and above, panoramic view of the complex.

Next pages, the project was designed to create the first great mountain development with a golf course in Mexico with the basic idea of conserving the beauty of the environment.

External and internal views of the rooms. All the spaces were designed according to the basic concept and premise of integrating local material into the form and function of the interior space.

Above, view of the House Club
patio.
Opposite page, chillout room.

Fiesta Americana Merida

Merida, Yucatan, Mexico

Completion date
1994

Owner
Desarrollo Comercial del Sudeste, s.a. de c.v.

Architect
GVA & Associates

Interior design
Arquitectura de Interiores

Engineering
GVA & Associates

The Fiesta Americana Merida complex consists of the Fiesta Americana Hotel and a 9,000-square-meter shopping mall.

It is located on an approximately 14,000-square-meter triangular plot of land pointing at one of the main avenues in Merida, where the best examples of turn of the 20th century architecture can be found. A building from that era is conserved on the property and integrated into the complex as a guideline for the project's plastic physiognomy. Special attention was given to integrating the complex into its surroundings since it is in the historic downtown area of Merida.

This integration was achieved by developing the hotel more horizontally with an attempt not to exceed the prevailing heights in the area.

Furthermore, the architecture of the complex responds to the character of the surrounding buildings, thus accomplishing great urban harmony.

The shopping mall, located on the ground floor of the complex, is integrated with the existing building as part of the project.

The 5-star hotel was built over the shopping mall; the first level houses public areas and a convention area. Above this level there are rooms distributed over five stories that give shape to an atrium. The public areas including the main lobby are covered by a spectacular stained glass dome at the top level.
A casual restaurant, a specialty restaurant, the lounge bar and a large terrace for events have an impressive view of the ancient avenue.

The convention area includes a large room that can hold up to 1,000 people and can be divided into 4 smaller rooms, 6 meeting rooms and a business center. This area also houses a Business Club that serves local entrepreneurs.

The hotel has 357 rooms, 22 executive suites and one presidential suite.

The 65,000-square-meter complex has a 23,000-square-meter underground parking garage for 550 cars, 9,000 sq.m for the shopping mall, and 32,500 for the hotel.

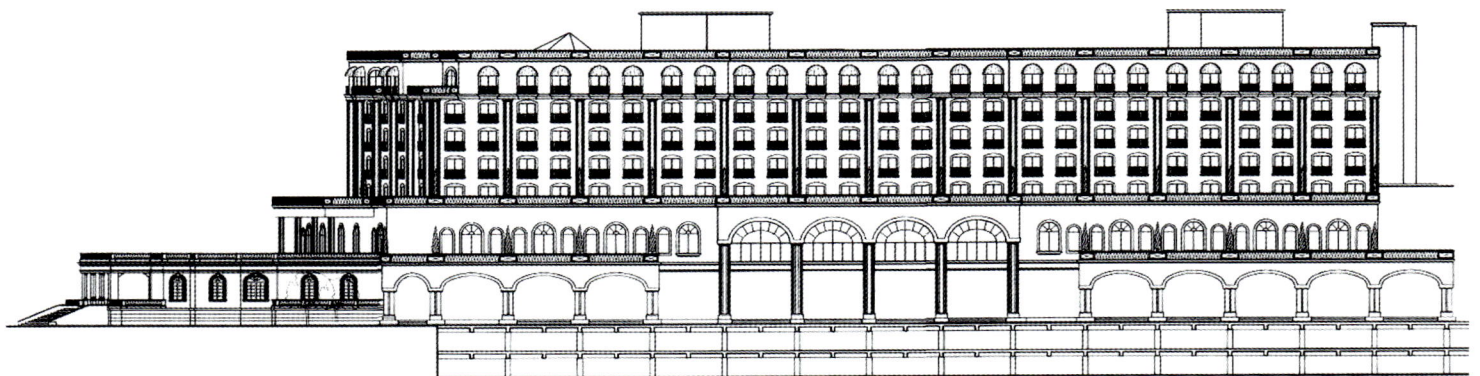

Main elevation.

Above, main facade of the
refurbished property.
Opposite page, view of the indoor
facade and pool.

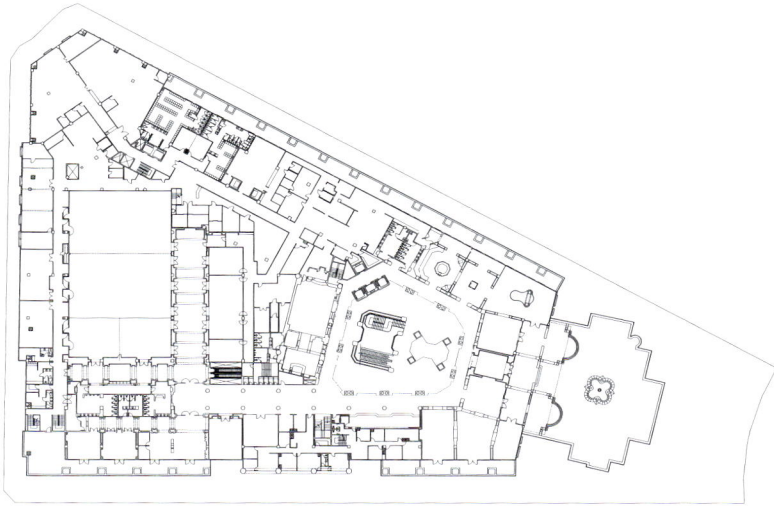

Retail center plan.

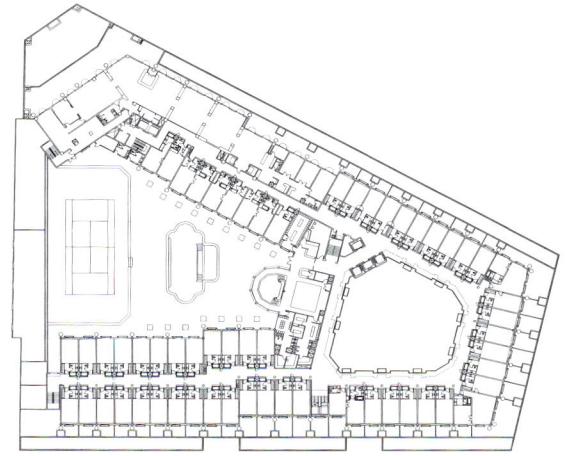

Typical rooms plan.

Opposite page, view of the lobby which is covered by a spectacular stained glass dome at the top level.

Top left, view of the lobby.
Top right, convention hall corridor.
Above, view of the bar lounge.

NORTE

PERIFERICO

INGRESO ALTERNO

NODO VIAL

LIMITE DEL TERRENO

BOULEVARD ATLIXCAYOTL

VISTA A LOS VOLCANES

INGRESO PRINCIPAL

HOTEL
COMERCIO
OFICINAS

AL CENTRO URBANO DE PUEBLA

RIO ATOYAC

CAMPO DE GOLF
18 HOYOS

CASA CLUB

CAMPO PRINCIPAL

APTOS.

TOWN HOUSES

APTOS.

LAGO

La Vista Country Club

Puebla

Completion date
September, 1997

Owner
**Dip. Desarrolladora Inmobiliaria de Puebla,
s.a. de c.v.**

Planning, urban design & architecture
GVA & Associates

Landscape Design
Peridian de México

Interior design
Arquitectura de Interiores

Golf course design
Robert Vonn Hagge

Engineering
GVA & Associates

La Vista is a self-sufficient sustainable residential development built over 131.67 hectares, with an 18 hole PGA category golf course. It is located on the outskirts of Puebla on the way to the highway to the south, about 9 kilometers from downtown.

The land is a valley with rolling hills crossed by three creeks that empty into the Atoyac River. The scenery is spectacular, particularly to the west with the majestic presence of the Popocatepetl and Iztaccihuatl volcanoes looming up on the horizon.

In order to integrate the La Vista development into the natural surroundings and the existing urban infrastructure, an exhaustive analysis of the site was made, including everything related to topography, hydrography, vegetation, soil, subsoil, scenery as well as the features of the adjacent urban areas.

The development has areas for single family dwellings, apartments, townhouses, the golf course clubhouse and a community center built over a total surface area of 69.25 hectares. 11.06 hectares have been set aside for streets, 2.11 for landscaping and communal areas, and 45.72 hectares for the golf course.

A basic objective of the urban design is to elevate the quality of life of the development's residents.

Therefore, the following was proposed:

minimize earth movements, keep the existing trees, reforest the streets and avenues abundantly, design a rolling street grading giving pedestrians the right of way, also integrating it into the landscape, establish a low construction density, install all utilities underground;

encourage community life with different facilities and leisure activities in the development such as the golf course, clubhouse, sports courts and pedestrian walkways, amongst other things;

use regional material and handicrafts; therefore, the fence that encircles the development was made out of adobe (raw clay bricks). Avenues have ornamental borders and geometric drawings made of pebbles and thin flagstone. Traffic circles are built around fountains and gardens with high quality visual elements;

preserve the ecological environment by treating and reusing waste water in the irrigation system, and separate garbage collection for recycling purposes, etc.;

offer residents an intelligent development with the most sophisticated security systems besides the manned and automatic control of the development's two entrances;

offer developers enough flexibility by designing a series of clusters that permit step-by-step growth according to real estate market behavior, thereby assuring the sales and occupation of the development in a short span of time.

The development, one of the best in Mexico, has been a complete success. The first stage opened in November 1998 and was completely sold by mid-2000.

The second stage is currently up for sale, while the last two stages are being programmed until all have been sold.

Above, view of the house club from
the golf course.
Opposite page from left, view of the
main entrance; detail of the house
club.

Opposite page, detail of the house club.

Top, aerial view of the main entrance.
Above, view of the patio.

Centro Magno

Guadalajara

Completion date
November, 1998

Owner
ICA Inmobiliaria

Architect
GVA & Associates

Centro Magno, a shopping mall and entertainment center built on a 12,000-square-meter piece of land located in a high-rent commercial area, is considered part of the historic downtown area of Guadalajara.

The original architectural concept was to build a project that would become the main development of its type in the city, that would project an architectural image with its own personality and yet identify with the urban and cultural context of Guadalajara.

The main components of the project are the following:

a three-level shopping mall and entertainment center with 65 different size premises and a total of 22,000 rentable sq.m of space;

a three-level underground parking garage that holds up to 1,100 cars, connected to the mall by stairs and escalators;

existing structure and installations for a 220 room all-suite hotel (a future stage) which will have a convention center, business center, spa and cafeteria.

The plaza style entrances to the building from each of the main arteries lead to a three-story high atrium crowned with an aluminum and laminated tempered glass dome. Commercial corridors fan out from the atrium as well as vertical circulation with escalators distributed to invite clients to flow around the entire mall, but with the central atrium as the focal point.

There are four restaurants, a café, a bar, a Hard Rock Live entertainment and concert complex as well as specialty shops on the ground floor. The hotel entrance will be from outside this ground floor; the hotel will begin at the third level of the mall.

Access and exit ramps from the parking garage, as well as loading and unloading docks, emergency exits etc., are all located on the side streets.

There are two restaurants, a cafeteria, a bar and discotheque upstairs as well as boutiques and shops.

The third level, besides other shops, holds a fast food court, a video arcade and a two-story movie theater complex with 19 theaters and 3,900 stadium style seats. The movie theater concept is open plan allowing mall customers have free access to the snacks counter and café.

At a cost of 25 million dollars with 70,000 sq.m of construction, Centro Magno opened in November 1998.

Above, night view of the building.
Opposite page, view of the Hard
Rock Concert Auditorium facade.

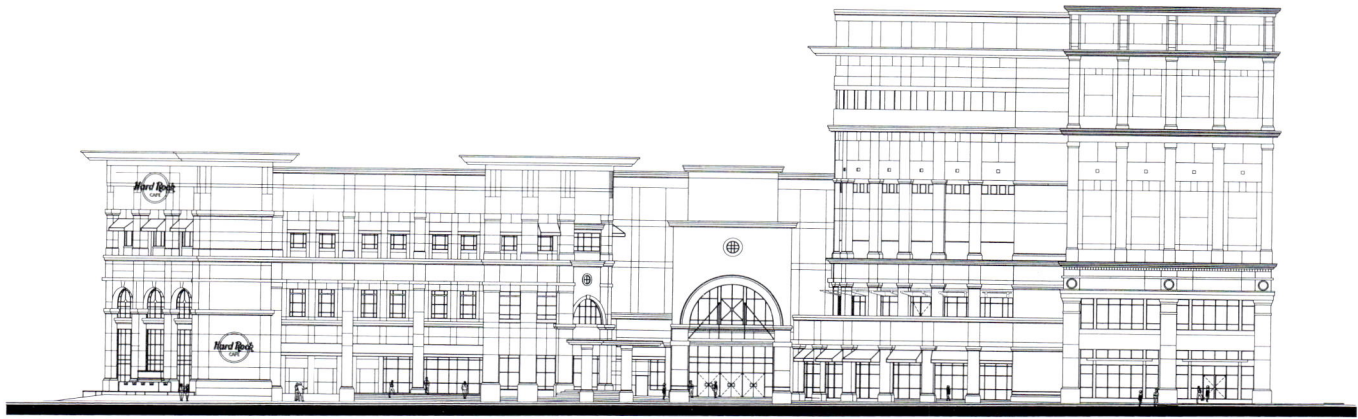

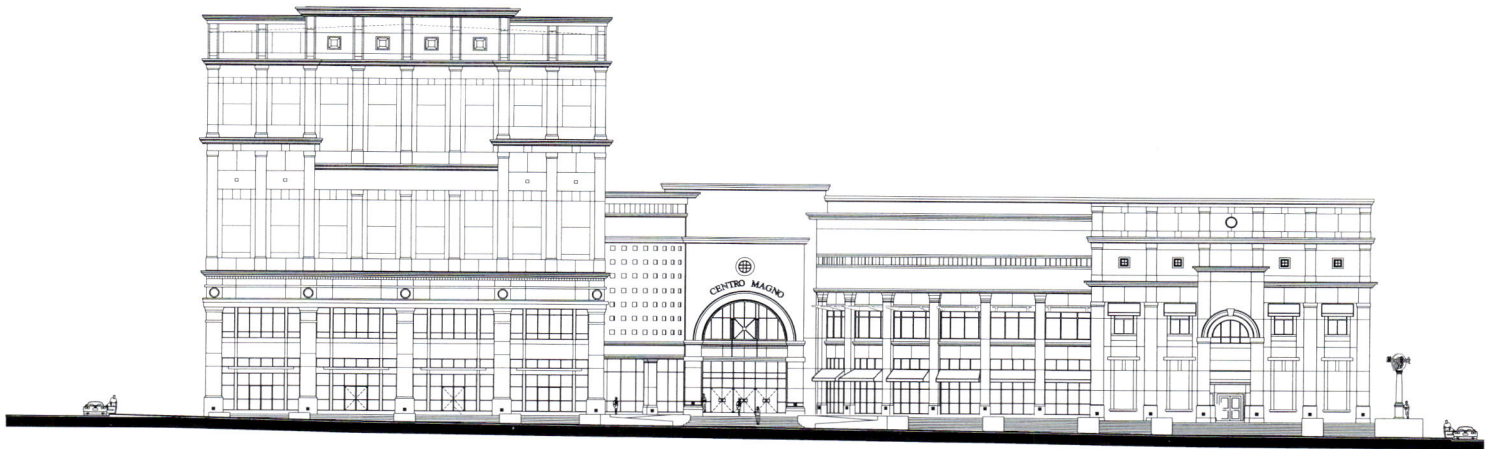

Main elevations.

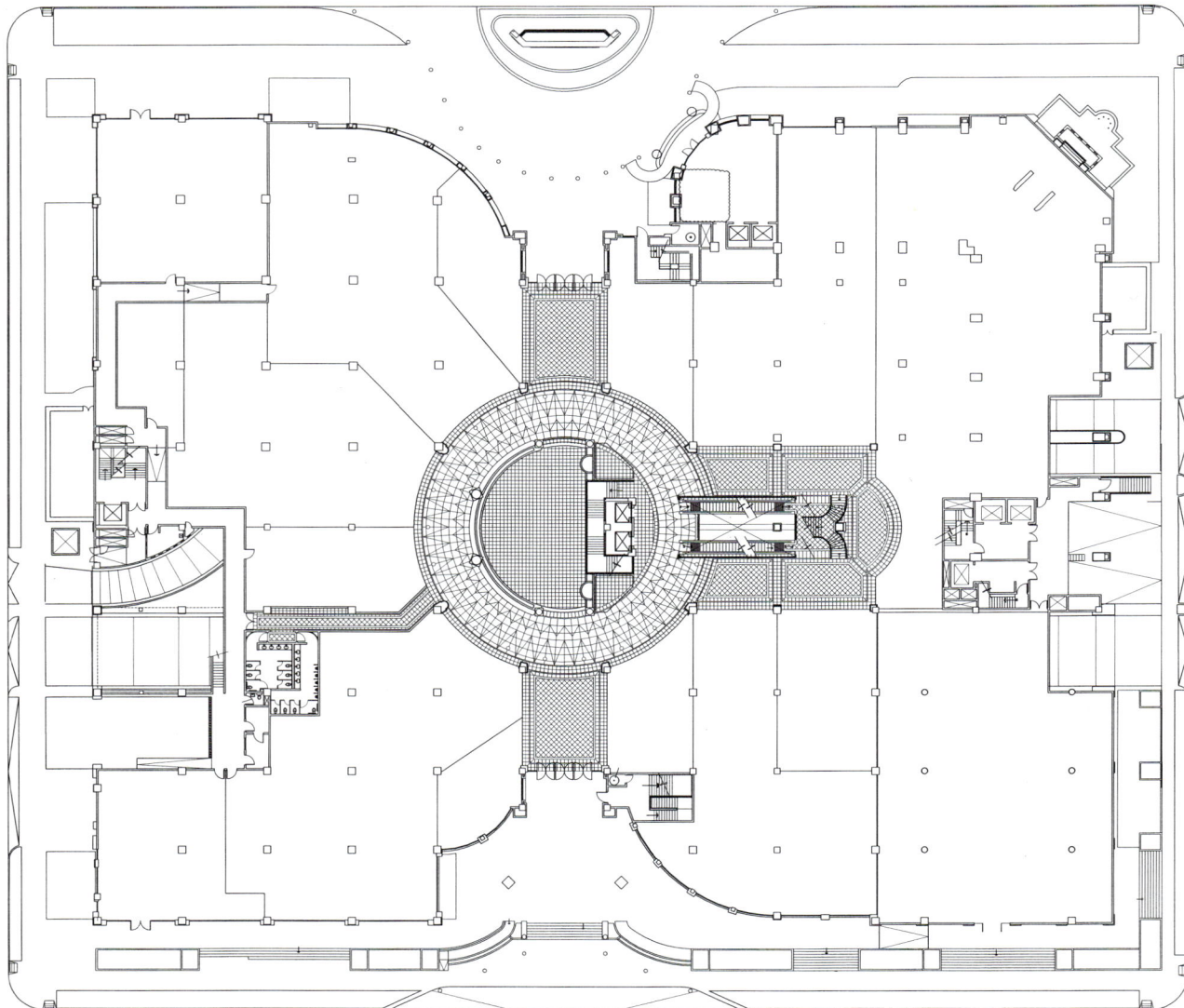

Main floor plan.

Opposite page, view of the elevators and the main dome. Above, view of the atrium from the third floor.

Isla Dorada

Cancun

Completion date
November, 1999

Owner
ICA Inmobiliaria

Architect
GVA & Associates

Landscape Design
Peridian de México

Interior design
Arquitectura de Interiores

Engineering
GVA & Associates

Isla Dorada is a modern residential concept with a Master Plan that complements human and environmental values.

It has been developed along the lines of excellence in a privileged area in the heart of the hotel zone of Cancun, Quintana Roo, facing the incomparable Mexican Caribbean.

Located between the Nichupte and Bojorquez lagoons and facing a golf course, Isla Dorada is a group of small islands connected by four splendid navigable canals.

Developed over a 56-hectare piece of land, it is divided into 12 clusters holding mansions, houses, villas, single dwelling and condominium lots, as well as a shopping area.

The idea was to make the development eco-friendly and sustainable, drawing on modern technology for treating sewage later used to water gardens, as well as proper garbage collection facilities.

The 3-kilometer-long interior avenue meandering its circular way throughout the development with the symbolic name of Paradise Avenue crosses the canals over bridges.

The roadway is made of cobblestones while a 6-meter-wide garden walkway runs along either side, turning it into a seamless park.

The clusters hold individual lots measuring from 300 to 650 sq.m. Each cluster has its own club house, swimming pool and complete utilities.

One of the clusters has been reserved for building 125 townhouses designed with two or three levels and two or three bedrooms. Surface areas range from 127 to 228 sq.m.

The town house design was made for eleven structures, some on the shores of the lagoon and others in a horseshoe configuration with a swimming and wading pool and leisure areas built in the middle.

All town houses were designed to afford a view of the beautiful Nichupte lagoon.

With regards to prototypes, six single family house projects were designed to be built on any of the individual lots distributed throughout the clusters. They were designed with two levels over surface areas ranging from 220 to 250 sq.m.

There are also prototypes of smaller houses that may be built on any of the individual lots distributed throughout the development.

The main feature of these houses is that they can be built in two stages according to the owner's needs, with 99 to 161 sq.m completed during the first stage.

Schematic section.

Top, aerial view of the complex
which is located between the
Nichupte and Bojoquez lagoons.
Opposite page, view of the main
entrance.

Schematic section on the canal.

The complex is a modern residential
concept with a Master Plan that
combines human and environmental
values.

JW MARRIOT
CANCUN.

J.W. Marriott Hotel

Cancun

Completion date
April, 2001

Owner
Inverisones turisticas de Cancun

Architect
**GVA & Associates /
Guillermo Carrillo Arenas**

Engineering
**Guillermo Carrillo Arenas /
GVA & Associates**

Landscape Design
Peridian de México

Interior design
Arquitectura de Interiores

This special category hotel is located in the tourist zone of Cancun on a 32,888,55-square-meter lot in front of Ballenas Beach and the Caribbean Ocean, just 3 kilometers north of the "El Rey" archaeological site and 6 kilometers south of Point Cancun, with a constructed surface of 60,000 sq.m and 451 rooms.

The hotel design aims at satisfying the market demand for conventions and business; it has the capacity to hold over 2,000 people in different meeting areas.

The 12-level room tower prevails architecturally; this concentration of the rooms allows for more spacious outside areas with its exuberant vegetation. There are 3 swimming pools, fishponds, and an area for snorkeling. A distinguishing feature is a reproduction of the coral reef with its tropical fish integrated into the specialty restaurant which will certainly be a popular attraction.

The hotel entrance is through a palm grove located between the property and Kukulkan Boulevard; this area is also used to enter the property through a garden. Landscaping is also used to hide an electrical substation located in the palm grove from guest visibility. The access plaza and motor lobby lead through to the main lobby where there is a view across a stretch of the Caribbean Ocean. The lobby lounge with its excellent ocean view is in front of the main lobby at a lower level.

South of the lobby there is a convention and business center area, the room tower and a casual restaurant as well as a world-class fitness center.

The specialty restaurant is north of the lobby as is the shopping area and Buddha Bar, a world-class restaurant belonging to the same chain found in Los Angeles, California, and Paris.

Hotel services are located in the basement level with an access that runs parallel to the northern property limit.

The convention center includes a ballroom that seats up to 1,200 people and an event patio for outdoor receptions with an impressive ocean view, also catering for 1,200 people.

The business center has a reception area, a sitting room, a library, 7 meeting rooms and 2 board rooms.

The room tower has 374 typical rooms, 43 junior suites, 28 bedsitting suites, 3 hospitality suites, 2 presidential suites and one vice-presidential suite.

Conceptual sketch of the facade.

Previous pages, aerial view of the hotel from the Caribbean Ocean.

Above, view of the whole complex which is located just three kilometres from "El Rey" archaeological site.

Opposite page, view of the facade from one of the three pools.

Mayan Palace
Guadalajara

Completion date
January, 2001

Owner
Mayan Resorts

Architect
GVA & Associates

Mayan Palace Guadalajara is a multi-purpose project combining a hotel and financial center in a 122,500-square-meter complex of which 24,700 sq.m are built on.

The work is located in a mixed business and commercial area.

The project comprises a theme hotel holding ample interior spaces with rich landscaping.

For the client, its main feature is:

"A long term profitable project, highly functional, easy to operate and quite comfortable. It highlights spatial quality and an abundance of light, allowing the creation of a truly comfortable and cozy ambiance. All this, wrapped in a unique, lasting somber elegance."

The architectural handling of volumes accomplishes an integration of use and image at the intersection between the financial center and the hotel building, resulting in a complex that shows personality.

The 50,000-square-meter, 14-level hotel houses 516 rooms, 2 presidential suites, 3 restaurants, 1 cafeteria, a lobby bar and a night club.

There is a convention hall that seats up to 1,000 people besides the meeting rooms, business center, spa, tennis courts, swimming pools and shop area.

One enters the ground floor down a wide interior driveway that leads to the financial center and, surrounded by gardens and fountains, reaches the motor lobby and main hotel lobby. This point is connected to the remaining public areas.

A large garden was designed for the rear side as part of the restaurant and cafeteria atmosphere. There is also an esplanade here for hosting outside events.

The room tower actually consists of two towers in a horseshoe layout with two wings to make everything work more smoothly. The upper levels are connected to the financial center, where the office penthouses are joined to an executive floor and the hotel's presidential suites.

The service area has a truck yard and a machine room, maintenance area, the kitchen, laundry, storehouse, employee services and business offices. This is all concentrated in a semi-basement level with its own entrance.

The 25,000-square-meter business center is located at the front of the property with a motor lobby and its own entrance at street level with access ramps in and out of the parking structure.

The 12 levels of office space with variable staggered surface areas following a vertical, circular line that allows each level to have a front terrace overlooking the avenue, thus producing both pleasant interior spaces and a dynamic exterior image. This is complemented by a two-level underground parking area holding up to 1,512 cars with direct exit to the avenue as well as to the interior driveway to the hotel and office building motor lobby with efficient vehicular flow.

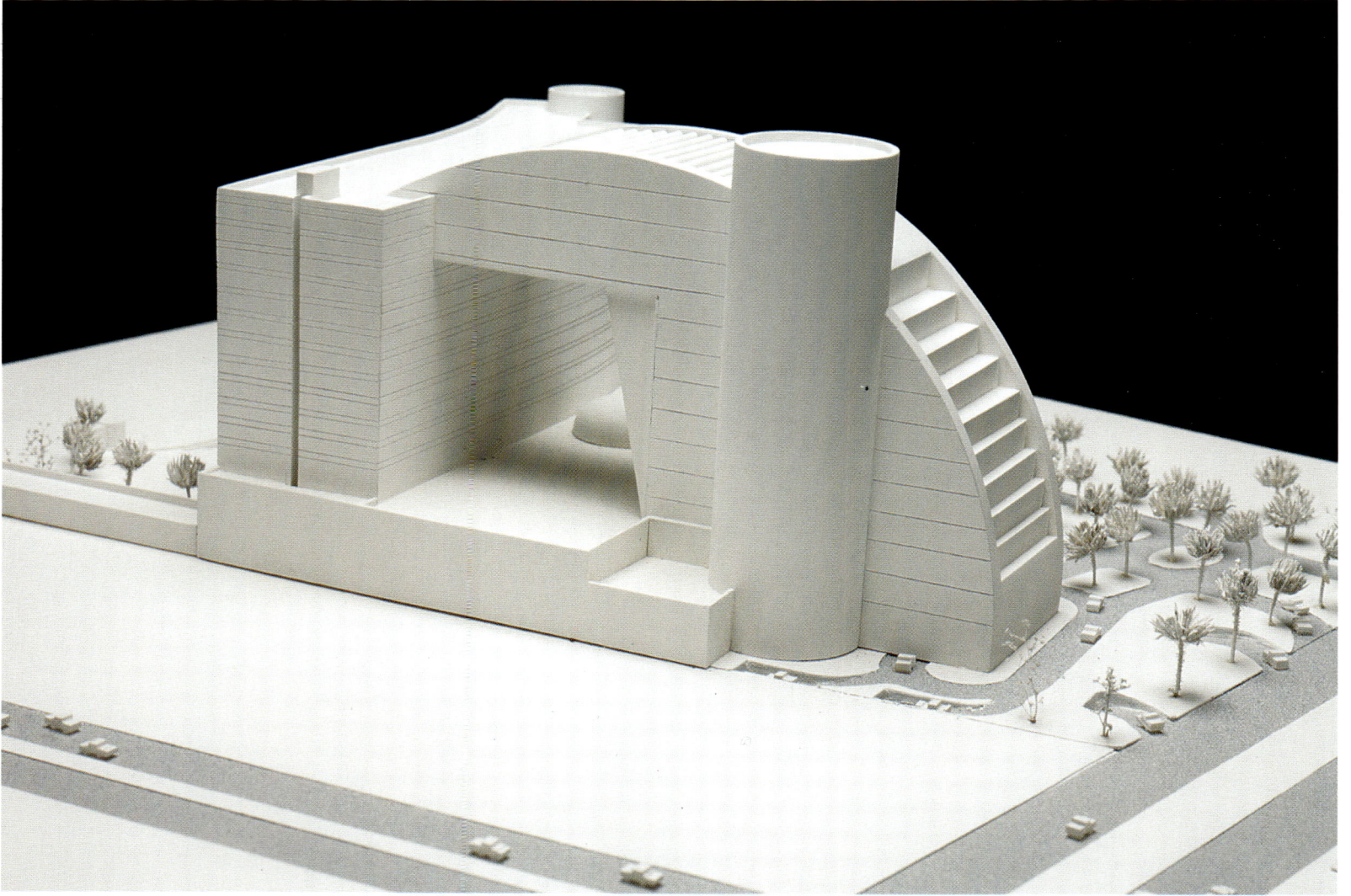

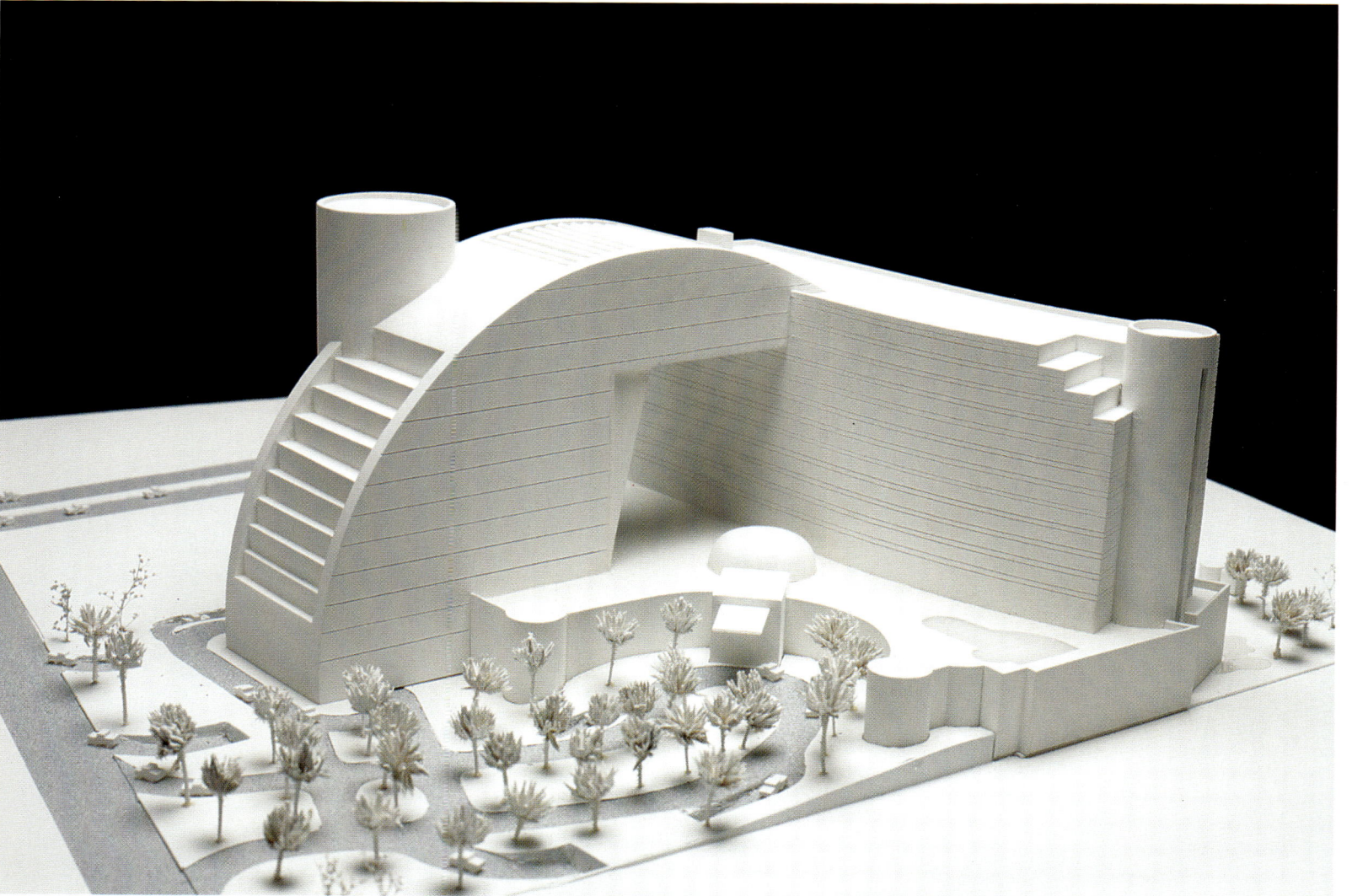

Lobby floor plan.

Opposite page, Mayan Palace is a
multi-purpose project combining a
hotel and a financial center.

Longitudinal section.

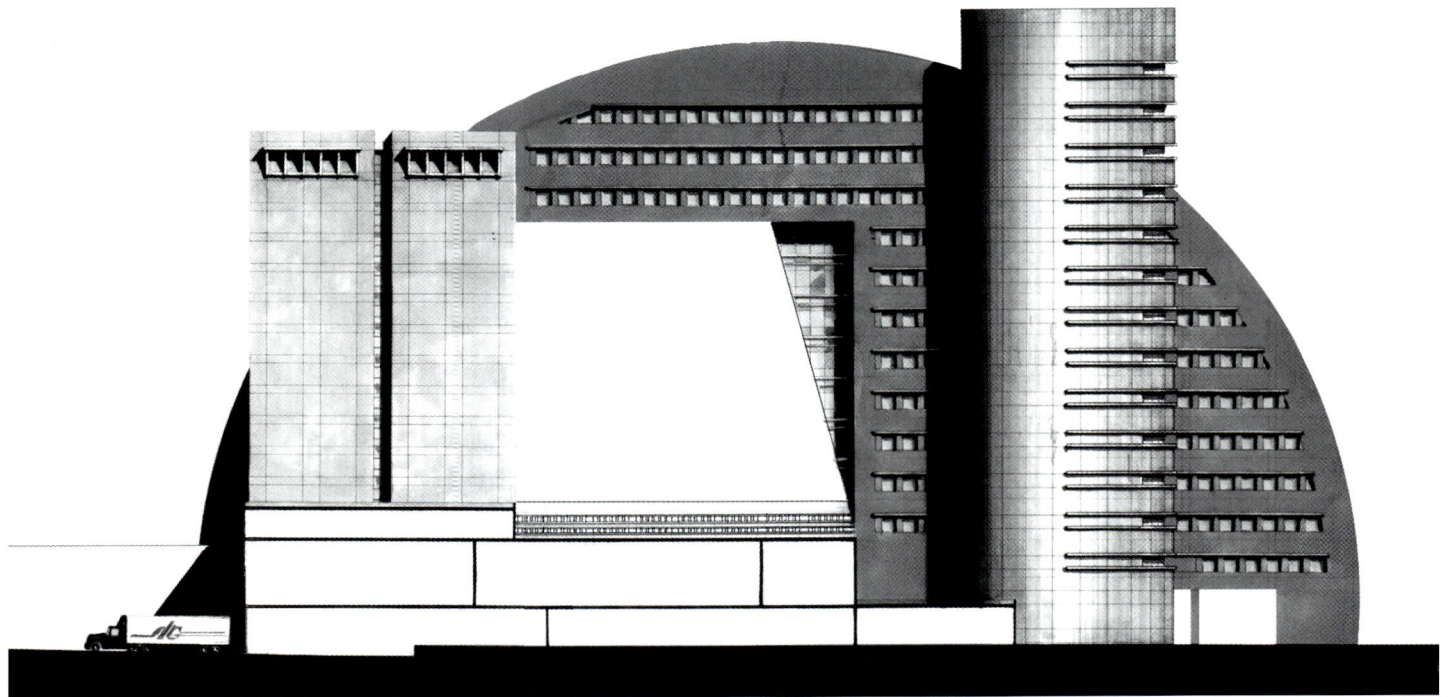

Side elevation.

Opposite page, the architectural combination of volumes accomplishes an integration of use and image at the intersection between the financial center and the hotel building.

Parque Milenium

Puebla

Completion date
February, 2001

Owner
Auchan Mexicana

Architect
GVA & Associates

Landscape Design
Peridian de México

The city of Puebla, located in the state of the same name, is currently one of the main metropolises in Mexico, offering a wide variety of attractions ranging from its archaeological, architectural and cultural heritage, recognized as part of the Patrimony of Humanity, to its modernity with a great urban infrastructure, modern shopping malls, hotels, residential developments with golf courses, besides its extraordinary natural surroundings.

The goal of Parque Milenium is to become the most important entertainment and shopping center in the city of Puebla. It was built on a 74,893.21-square-meter plot of land in the far eastern part of the city at the crossroads of one of the main avenues leading to other nearby towns and the city's peripheral highway.

The essence of the project was to handle monumental spaces below spectacular aluminium and glass domes on a wood structure covered with a Teflon membrane, and to handle new designs on the floors as well as in the false ceilings with special lighting that achieves unique effects.

The Parque Milenium Shopping Mall and Entertainment Center Project consists mainly of: one hypermarket, seven anchor stores and 85 locales spread over two stories; one outdoor parking area for the Mall with 466 car capacity; one indoor parking structure for the Mall with 1,356 car capacity; corporate building with a capacity for 32 offices with 400 square meters each; five indoor parking structures with a 393 car capacity.

The project for 13,311.04 sq.m total construction was developed over three levels, following the shore of the Atoyac River as well as the surrounding streets.

Access to the outdoor parking lot is from the avenue while the exit leads to the Peripheral Highway. There are two entrances to the mall at each level as well as from the parking basement.

The shopping mall has a curved layout with premises on either side. The mall entrances also lead to the hypermarket which has a loading dock and a truck yard with a separate entrance.

One of the mall wings along the avenue has a two-level entertainment center as well as a fast food courtyard on the lower level with ample seating and tables. There is also a two-story ice-skating rink with a spectacular elliptic dome covered with a Teflon membrane and supported by laminated wooden trusses.

The mall has public service areas and strategically located emergency exits pursuant to the building code. There is also a 15-story corporate building in the project with a two-story-high lobby with entrances from the basement, the motor lobby and the parking structures.

Each level of the corporate building has all services and a vestibule in the elevator area. Parque Milenium opened in February 2001.

Above, exterior view of the Auchan
stores.
Opposite page from top, detail of
the exterior lighting; view of the
shopping center.

Top, view of the Trav-e-lator and false ceiling lighting.

Above, night view of the main entrance.

Opposite page, view of the Teflon dome and the ice skating rink.

Secrets Punta Cana
The Dominican Republic

Completion date
September, 2004

Owner
Paloma Investments Group

Architect
GVA & Associates

Landscape
Peridian de Mexico

Interior design
Arquitectura de Interiores

Graphic-environmental design
Idée

Engineering
GVA & Associates

This project is located in a mangrove thicket at Punta Cana in the Dominican Republic. Punta Cana has been the area with most developments in the Caribbean over the last few years.
Swamp conditions forced us to raise the buildings on landfill because the soil load capacity is quite poor. The 30-hectare property has enabled us to develop the buildings horizontally, give the public areas sea views, and still preserve an almost 20-hectare environmental reserve.

The 5-star hotel holds 367 rooms with a view of the Caribbean Ocean, each with a panoramic Jacuzzi, a terrace and small living room. 34 master suites have ocean views, a panoramic Jacuzzi, a terrace and a living room while the presidential suite has a kitchenette, living room, dining room, and two Jacuzzis, for a total of 402 rooms.

The project also includes five different specialty restaurants, a spa, sports courts, a theater, shops, a kids club, swimming pools and other outdoor attractions.
The hotel architecture is a mild blend of construction elements with a Mediterranean-Caribbean flavor in its colors, materials and shapes, giving it an up-to-date look combining thatched roofs, thick walls, straight columns, tiles, washed cement floors and stone friezes, producing the spirit of a modern elegant complex, quite the thing for relaxation, romance and fun.

A soft trail leads from the entrance into a spectacular plaza surrounded by a lake buried in vegetation, while a reflecting pool in the middle of the plaza governs circulation.

A bridge from the motor lobby spans the lake and leads to the lobby, a spectacular thatched building where there are no construction elements to block the ocean view through thick vegetation.
The building, housing a theater, a lounge bar and an American restaurant, is set out around a palm tree plaza that serves as a point of reference since it distributes the flow of guests to the different restaurants: American, Italian, Oriental, the beach restaurant and the main one, all of which have been designed with their own special ambiance created by the architecture and reinforced by the decoration, thus offering guests different atmospheres and experiences.

Rooms are found in two large clusters, each divided into four, bridge-connected buildings, thereby articulating the buildings while minimizing large continuous spaces. Each cluster features a pool in the middle for relaxation purposes.

Each room measures 38 sq.m, has an ocean view, and even first level rooms are raised at least a meter and a half above ground level. Each room has a small living room, terrace, a Jacuzzi with an ocean view and an entrance from the bathroom as well as from the bedroom or terrace.

The master suites are found at the front of each wing of rooms; they have the same features as the rooms but spread over 55.6 sq.m, a formal living room and a larger bathroom.
The 110-square-meter presidential suite has a foyer, living and dining room, a kitchenette with a service entrance, a terrace with hammocks and a panoramic Jacuzzi in addition to the one in on-suite bathroom. This suite can be extended by adding on a master suite which can also be used separately.

Altogether, the hotel offers a range of possibilities and daytime/nighttime activities in an integrated, elegant atmosphere, enabling it to become one of the most important hotels in the Caribbean.

Above from top, view of the motor
lobby; elevation of the rooms
building.

Site plan. Punta Cana has been the area with most developments in the Caribbean over the last few years.

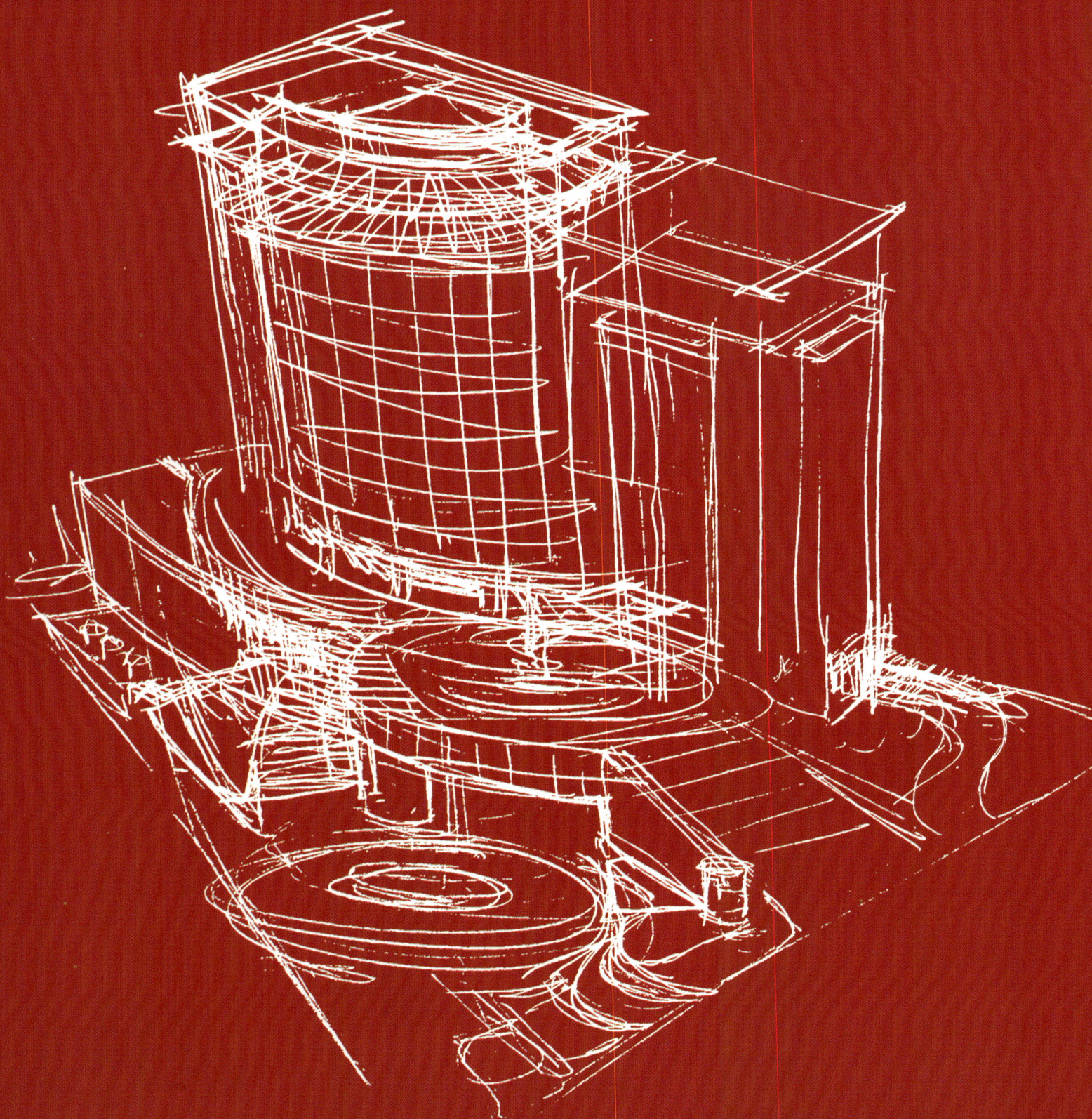

Plaza Marine - Novotel

Santa Fè

Completion date
December, 2001

Owner Hotel
Accor

Owner Corporate Offices
Jar Estate Corp

Architect
GVA & Associates

Landscape Design
Peridian de México

Interior design
Arquitectura de Interiores

Engineering
GVA & Associates

The southwestern area of Mexico City holds what was once one of the most densely populated parts of town but is currently very much an entrepreneurial zone: Santa Fè.

Plaza Marine in Santa Fè is one of the newest buildings constructed in this area of wealth, tradition, and rising property values, now one of the most modern parts of Mexico City.

Here, where corporate buildings housing some of the most important local and international companies are concentrated alongside the most exclusive shops, Santa Fè has not only become a select area for companies and shopping, but also an after-office-hours meeting place for up-and-coming young executives with its exclusive restaurants and entertainment.

Close to one of the city's largest and most important malls, next to one of the most traditional universities, the Ibero-Americana, it is also not far from the exclusive residential areas in the Bosques de las Lomas area, and about 25 minutes from Polanco and 40 kilometers from the International Airport.

Plaza Marine began as an interesting concept in multiple uses. Developed on a 4,000-square-meter lot, bordering on two other lots, a pedestrian walkway, with only one side facing the street, one of the first problems to be solved were the entrances and exits to and from the parking garage, as well as two motor lobbies since a third business, a restaurant that is separate from the hotel and corporate building, has its own motor lobby.

The Plaza Marine multi-purpose building with a total of 32,000 sq.m of buildings houses a nine-story corporate building with a little over 800 sq.m per floor, and a 148-room business class hotel belonging to the French Accor chain under the commercial name of Novotel.

Among other attractions, it has an entire floor of meeting rooms, a cafeteria, bar, and a terrace on the top level with a pool, snack bar and gym.

There is also a six-level underground parking garage that holds up to 514 cars while respecting the zoning standards with regards to the number of parking spaces due to the diversity of uses within the building.

It is worth mentioning that state-of-the-art technology for a triple A building was adopted for the engineering, protection, special installations, and so forth.

Opposite page, view of the facade.
Plaza Marine is one of the newest
buildings constructed in this area.

Pueblo Bonito Punta Mita

Puerto Vallarta

Completion date
2003

Owner
Pueblo Bonito Hoteles & Resorts

Architect
GVA & Associates

Interior Design
Arquitectura de Interiores

Landscape design
Peridian de Mexico

Engineering
GVA & Associates

Graphic - environmental design
Idée

This important project is being developed on 13.95 hectares in the Banderas Bay area of Puerto Vallarta, one of the fastest growing tourism areas in Mexico.

The property has about 320 meters of beach front with quite abundant vegetation.

Due to the particular characteristics of "Pueblo Bonito" hotels requiring an ambitious program that takes into account a large amount of time-sharing units and a hotel in the same development, the project was zoned into three large areas covering a total constructed area of 83,000 sq.m.

The first such area is the public area building, immediately identifiable with its 40 meter high 50 meter long thatched roof; this is the main reception area of the development.

This impressive building includes guest services such as group reception, development sales, bar, speciality restaurant, ballroom, meeting room, shop area and a large spa with 29 individual rooms for body treatments and relaxation.

The second area is the main product of the development consisting of a group of buildings housing 557 time-sharing units.

These are two and four story buildings distributed in clusters around their own recreation areas such as swimming pools, sundecks, a snack bar and steakhouse.

In each and every one of these buildings, the premise that each guest has an ocean view from his/her room as well as from the restaurants and pools has been kept. This area has three types of rooms: one-bedroom master suites with a lounge area; one bedroom junior suites; and some honeymoon suites overlooking the surrounding scenery according to their location. They have a terrace, Jacuzzi, one bedroom, two full bathrooms and a very comfortable living room.

A certain harmony has been achieved in this complex by mixing contemporary elements with regional materials. Facades were designed with a mixture of curves and straight lines permitting a certain play of light and shade according to the position of the sun, that together with the earth tones coming from the sloping roofed buildings create a very pleasant visual sensation.

The third area is for a 100-suite hotel with a very pleasant architectural design. The bedroom and the Jacuzzi in the bathroom have a direct ocean view. The hotel is in the most privileged corner of the development, towards the cliff overlooking the sea and entire bay.

Not unlike the above mentioned complex, a very special play of light and shade was accomplished by breaking the rhythm of the facade with a geometrically very clean thatched area housing the lobby and front desk and a view inviting guests to admire the bay and Puerto Vallarta.

The hotel area has recreation areas, restaurants offering three meals a day under a thatched roof, and partially covered terraces to contemplate the different views available at this spot.

There are 10 suites next to this building, each with its own swimming pool and very special ambiences and spaces that give the sensation of being free while enjoying privacy, due to the open link between the interior spaces with the terraces and gardens.

The development has a sports area located over the machine room for playing tennis and paddleball in a space adequately air-conditioned for playing these sports.

It also offers all the services expected of this kind of tourist development, making it one of the most important and complete developments in the region.

Site plan.

Opposite page from top, views of
the lake and the honey moon suites.
Facades have a mixture of straight
and curved lines permitting a certain
play of light and shade.

Opposite page from top, views of
the entrance and retails area.
Above, view of the lake.

Contemporary elements and
regional materials have been mixed
in this harmonious complex.

Sanctuary of the Martyrs

Guadalajara

Completion date
2004

Owner
Fundacion El Fruto de los Santos

Architect
GVA & Associates

Mexico is a country united around centuries-old religious roots. The main show of faith takes place on December 12th each year in commemoration of our Lady of Guadalupe, also known as the patron of the Americas.

Twenty-three priests and three laymen, Mexican martyrs, were declared saints in Rome in the year 2000.

In view of the devotion the faithful profess to these martyrs for their exemplary worthiness, a project was set under way in Guadalajara known as the Sanctuary of the Martyrs.

The thinking was that a monument would suffice for honoring the martyrs. But precisely because the martyrs had close ties with Guadalajara, they decided in favor of a Sanctuary-Auditorium with room for fifteen to twenty thousand people under an enormous cupola to give a religious character to the work. In front of this large spiritual congregation space there will be a plaza for holding outside ceremonies. There will also be a church for holding daily Mass, and meeting rooms for congresses and conventions, serving the whole of Mexico.

The project will consist of a main floor holding a 250 by 125 meter atrium, and a 6.25 meter long, 10 meter high indoor colonnade. The bell tower will be 80 meters high with a belfry for 72 bells, there will also be a watchtower that can be climbed up two elevators or stairs, topped by a cross with a 36 meter high, 24 meter wide sculpture of the Resurrected Christ.

The main entrance will be monumental, 50 meters wide, covered by the Great Papal Box 14 meters above the main floor. There will be two side entrances, one in the north and the other in the south, through the colonnade surrounding the Sanctuary.

The main nave will be surrounded by gardens and open aisles that will be like vestibules, from the main as well as the side entrances, with vertical circulation leading upstairs. Total capacity will be for 20,000 seated people, 13,500 on the ground floor and 6,500 upstairs.

The 700-square-meter presbytery will also be monumental and capable of holding 250 men of cloth, including cardinals, bishops, monsignors and priests. There will be one altar and 2 pulpits for saying Mass. There will be sufficient space for ordaining 100 priests, a choir loft, and a loft for the philharmonic orchestra. The crowning touch of the presbytery will be a sculptured wall 36 meters wide and 21 meters high that will hold a series of sculptures and paintings along with a monumental Christ.

The cupola will divide the floor plan into four segments. The main nave will be 120 meters in diameter, the central copula 80 meters in diameter at a height of 80 meters. The cupola structure will be lined with a special amber-colored glass, laminated and tempered with an inside layer of PVB. The top of the cross will stand 135 meters tall.

Above, view of the main entrance.
The enormous cupola gives a
religious character to the work.

View of the atrium.

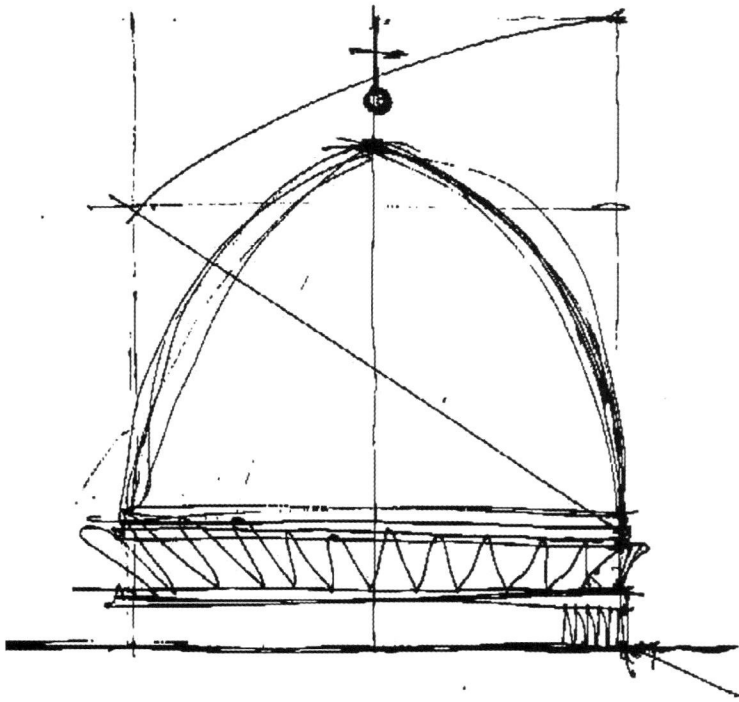

Preliminary sketch of the Dome.

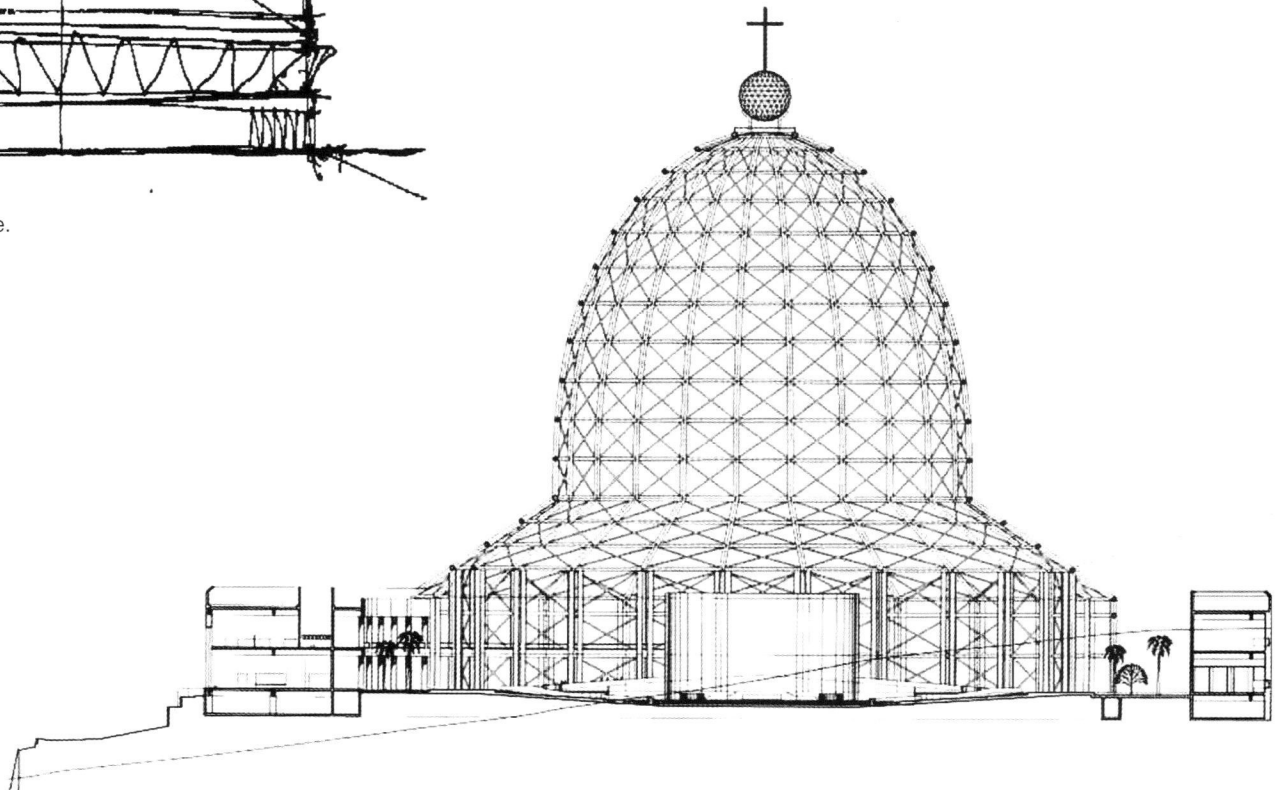

Longitudinal section of the Dome.

Mundo Mall

Santo Domingo

Completion date
November, 2004

Owner
Metropolitana Comercial

Architect
GVA & Associates

Landscape Design
Peridian de México

Interior design
Arquitectura de Interiores

The Mundo Mall, corporate building and hotel, located in the center of the Santo Domingo metropolitan area in the Dominican Republic, are part of the most ambitious and complex development in the Caribbean, and come to satisfy a number of the city's needs.

It consists of a three-level shopping mall with an ice-skating rink in the middle. It also has three corporate office towers, a 250-room 5-star hotel aimed mainly at businessmen including a ballroom, business center, outdoors pool and a jogging track among other services as well as a three-level underground parking garage.

The elements making up the project are developed on a 65,231 sq.m piece of property facing three of Santo Domingo's main avenues; therefore its integration into the surroundings is of great importance. Total constructed area of 404,853.79 sq.m is a true indication of this complex's impressive dimensions.

Entrances to the mall are on the ground floor from each of the avenues surrounding the property. The hotel and towers have separate entrances to the motor lobby and access plaza. They are connected by an internal street that runs along the front of the property with strategically located entrances and exits guaranteeing rapid exit by car. This was one of the main problems to be solved due to the large number of parking spaces required.

The ground floor shopping mall has a 12,300-square-meter supermarket besides other anchor and sub anchor stores and premises with varying surface areas. These are all connected along a large loop that at each end as well as in the entrances is covered by a three story high atrium with 25 meter diameter domes made out of glass and aluminum, besides the main attraction in the middle: an ice-skating rink under a Teflon membrane ceiling supported by a concrete and wooden structure.

There is a 5,000-square-meter anchor store upstairs located at the northwest end of the development as well as other sub anchor stores and shops. Furthermore, there are two restaurants near the front of the development, both affording views of the park-located kitty-corner.

On this same level there is a second plaza with a fourth atrium, a nucleus of escalators and stairs that lead to the movie theaters located up on the third level of the mall, which also has several anchor and sub anchor stores strategically located to achieve optimum commercial flow.

At this level we find a video arcade while there is a fast food and entertainment area located in the middle that includes 12 movie theaters.

The fourth level will have a 5,452-square-meter spa.

The mall is furbished with all the necessary services, such as separate loading and unloading docks, emergency stairwells, restrooms, service entrances, etc., to guarantee operations run smoothly.

The three office towers are another important aspect of the development; two of them will be 15 levels tall while the third one will be between 18 and 20 levels tall. Each tower will have a separate entrance and a service hub at each level.

A hotel was integrated into the development at the eastern end, its eight stories and main floor with public services rising from the top level of the mall. It has its own access at street level, its own motor lobby, access patio and service areas, as well as a direct entrance from the underground parking structure.

The hotel has a convention center for up to 800 people, a business center, meeting rooms, a casual restaurant, a specialty restaurant, as well as a swimming pool area with terraces.

The development has a three-level underground parking garage that can hold up to 5,600 cars and 920 motorcycles in different spots underground, since this means of transport is quite popular in the city of Santo Domingo.

The Mundo Mall consists of three-level shopping mall, three corporate office towers, hotel business center, pool, sports facilities and an underground parking garage.

List of Works

Planning

Puerto Iguana, Puerto Vallarta Jal.
Río San Juan de Dios, Guadalajara Jal.
Planificación Regional
de la Costa de Jalisco XAPAC XXI
Malecón Cancún, Cancún Q.R.
Cala Diamante Finestrat, Benidorm España
Nuevo Guanajuato, Guanajuato Gto.
Puerto Santiago, Manzanillo, Colima
Plan Verde Regional de Guadalajara
Plan estratégico regional de la Ribera de Chapala
Revisión Plan Maestro Los Cabos (Revisión)
Revisión Plan Maestro Cancún (Revisión)
Planificación Ribera de Chapala 2da Etapa
El Divisadero, Chihuahua, Chihuahua., (Fonatur)

Master Plans

Costa Careyes, Careyes, Jal.
Tlayacapan, Guadalajara, Jal.
Cd. Loma Dorada, Guadalajara, Jal.
Puerto Iguana, Puerto Vallarta, Jal.,
Marina Vallarta, Puerto Vallarta, Jal.,
Río San Juan de Dios, Guadalajara, Jal.
Villa San Sebastián, Guadalajara, Jal.
Sta. Ana del Colli, Guadalajara, Jal.
Marina Ixtapa, Ixtapa, Zihuatanejo, Gro.
Costalegre, Jalisco
Isla Dorada, Cancún, Q.R.
Malecón Cancún, Cancún, Q.R.
Cala Diamante Finestrat, Benidorm. España
Guanajuato Nuevo Horizonte, Guanajuato, Gto.
Marina Guaymas, Guaymas, Son.
Plan Maestro Náutico Isla Dorada, Cancún, Q.R.
Playa Bagdad, Tamaulipas
El Careño
Bosque Real II, México D.F.
Villa Panamericana, Guadalajara, Jalisco.
Isla Blanca, Quintana Roo.
Tlajomulco Zúñiga, Jalisco, concurso.
Centro Cultural
de la Universidad de Guadalajara, concurso.
Plan Maestro para Coamo Springs, Puerto Rico.

Urban Renovations

Zapopan, Zapopan, Jal.
Plaza Tapatia, Guadalajara, Jal.
Tuxtla Gutierrez, Chiapas.
Plaza Aguascalientes, Aguascalientes, Ags.
Tourist Developments (Selection)
Costa Careyes, Jalisco.
Los Tules, Puerto Vallarta Jal.
Marina Vallarta, Puerto Vallarta Jal.
Punta Coral, Cancún Q.R.
Isla Iguana, Puerto Vallarta Jal.
Puerto Iguana, Puerto Vallarta Jal.
San Francisco Palancar, Cancún Q.R.
Rancho Majagua, Manzanillo Col.
Club de Yates, Cabo San Lucas B.C.S.
Club Vacacional Marriott Vallarta,
Puerto Vallarta Jal.
Marina Ixtapa, Ixtapa-Zihuatanejo Gro
Isla Dorada, Cancún Q.R.
Puerto Santiago, Manzanillo, Colima.
Isla Blanca, Quintana Roo.
Urban and Residential Developments
Club de Golf Atlas, Guadalajara, Jal.
Real Vallarta, Guadalajara, Jal.
San Miguel de la Colina, Guadalajara, Jal.

Loma Blanca, Guadalajara, Jal.
Jardines de La Cruz, Guadalajara, Jal.
Cabañas Sta. Anita, Guadalajara, Jal.
Pueblo Careyitos, Careyes, Col.
Jardines de La Cruz, Guadalajara, Jal.
Jardines Del Sur, Guadalajara, Jal.
Camino Real, Guadalajara, Jal.
Santa Ruta, Guadalajara, Jal.
El Palomar, 2da Seccion, Guadalajara, Jal.
Ciudad Bugambillas,
2da Seccion, Guadalajara, Jal.
Rio San Juan De Dios, Guadalajara, Jal.
Residencial San Pedro, Guadalajara, Jal.
Club Campestre Y Residencial "El Cristo",
Atlixco Puebla
Pueblo Careyes, Careyes, Col.
Lomas Del Bosque, Guadalajara, Jal.
Jardines Universidad, Guadalajara, Jal.
Santa Ana Del Colli, Guadalajara, Jal.
Arce Desarrollo.
Villa San Sebastian, Guadalajara, Jal.
Villas Pitillal, Puerto Vallarta, Jal.
Villas Plaza Del Rio, Tijuana, B.C.N.
Arboledas, Guadalajara, Jal.
Loma Dorada, Guadalajara, Jal.
Fracc. 8 de Diciembre, Guadalajara, Jal.
Parque Regency, Guadalajara, Jal.
Parque de La Castellana, Guadalajara, Jal.
Callejon Del Parque, Guadalajara, Jal.
Condolago, Cancún, Q.R.
Villa Magna, Guadalajara, Jal.
Villa Coral, Guadalajara, Jal.
Isla Dorada, Cancún, Q.R.
Villas Carvi, Puerto Vallarta, Jal.
Villa Marbella, Guadalajara, Jal.
Club Hacienda, Tapalpa, Jal.
Villa Mallorca, Puerto Vallarta, Jal.
Puerta Del Sol, Puerto Vallarta, Jal.
Villas Del Country, Puerto Vallarta, Jal.
Casas Santa Lucia, Guadalajara, Jal.
Residencial Del Parque, Aguascalientes, Ags.
Clusters Ixtapa, Ixtapa, Gro.
Malecon Cancun, Cancún, Q.R.
Costa Club Villas, Cancún, Q.R.
Condominio Altavista, México, D.F.
Villas Isla Dorada, Cancún, Q.R.
Casas Isla Dorada, Cancún, Q.R.
Jardines Del Lago, Aguascalientes, Ags.
Lomas de San Angel, México, D.F.
Las Cañadas, Guadalajara, Jal.
Tapalpa Country Club, Tapalpa, Jal.
Guanajuato Nuevo Horizonte, Guanajuato, Gto.
Las Laborcilla, Queretaro, Qro.
Los Encinos, Zapopan, Jal.
Jardines Del Valle, Zapopan, Jal.
Nuevo San Isidro, Guadalajara Jal.
Puerta de Hierro Village, Guadalajara Jal.
Condominio Horizontal Arargo, Guadalajara Jal.
Reserva Sur Cancun, Cancún, Q.R.
Hacienda Los Cedros, Tlaquepaque, Jal.
Jardines Mixcoac, México, D.F.
Jardin Real, Zapopan Jal.
Pichilingue, Punta Diamante, Acapulco, Gro.
Puertas Del Tule, Zapopan, Jal.
La Cantera, Chihuahua, Chih.
Angelopolis, Puebla, Pue.
Residencial Santa Fe, México D. F.
Ajijic Country Club, Ajijic, Jal.
Residencial Los Aguacates, Cuernavaca, México.
Lomas San Angel Residencial
y Condominios, México, D.F.
Fraccionamiento Industrial, Zapopan, Jalisco.
Loma Real, Los Ocotes, Guadalajara, Jalisco.
Residencial San Jose Del Tajo,
Guadalajara, Jalisco.

Bosque Real Lotes 1,2,28,33,34,38 y 42,
México D.F.
Clusters 10,11,12,13,14,17
y 19 La Vista, Puebla, Pue.

Entertainment Buildings

Estadio Jalisco, ampliación, Guadalajara, Jal.
Plaza De Toros Nuevo Progreso,
Guadalajara, Jal.
Plaza De Toros, Mazatlán, Sin.
Salón de La Fama Para El Futbol Mexicano,
concurso, Guadalajara

Commercial and Entertainment Buildings

Plaza Americas, Guadalajara, Jal.
Plaza Mexico, Guadalajara, Jal., Aurrera.
Plaza Atemajac, Guadalajara, Jal., Aurrera.
Plaza Revolucion, Guadalajara, Jal., Aurrera.
Aurrera Irapuato, Irapuato, Gto.
Suburbia Zaragoza, México, D.F., proyecto.
Plaza Juarez, Cd. Juárez Chih, Soriana.
Soriana Constitucion, Torreón, Coah.
Soriana Torreon, Torreón, Coah.
Soriana Durango, Durango, Dgo.
Soriana Saltillo 400, Torreón Coah.
Soriana Monterrey, Monterrey, N. L.
Soriana Reynosa, Reynosa, Tamps.
Rio Tijuana, Tijuana, B.C.N.
Plaza Marina, Puerto Vallarta, Jal.
Soriana Juarez, Cd. Juárez, Chih.
Soriana nvo. Laredo, Tamps.
Plaza Cozumel, Cozumel, Q.R.
Plaza San Lucas, Cabo San Lucas, B.C.S.
Plaza Dorada, Cancún, Q.R.
Expo Plaza, Aguascalientes, Ags., Sanborns.
Plaza Loreto, México, D.F.
Plaza Bugambilias, Guadalajara, Jal.
Plaza Leon, León, Gto., Sanborns
Centro Comercial Merida, Mérida, Yuc.
Soriana Rio Nilo, Guadalajara Jal.
Centro Comercial Rio Sonora, Hermosillo, Son.
Centro Comercial, Costa Rica
Mexico Magico Isla Dorada, Cancún, Q. R.
Centro Queretaro. Querétaro Qro.
Soriana Plaza Juarez, Ciudad Juárez, Chih.
Soriana Centro Torreón, Torreón, Coah.
Soriana Tampico, Tampico, Tamps.
Soriana Juarez Ii, Ciudad Juárez Chih.
Centromagno, Centro de Entretenimiento,
Guadalajara.
El Pabellón, Centro Comercial
y Entretenimiento.
Centro Comercial y Entretenimiento, Leon.
Auchan, Puebla.

Mixed Use Buildings

Hotel Fiesta Americana y Centro Comercial,
Mérida, Yucatán.
Plaza Loreto, Centro Comercial
y de Entretenimiento, México D.F.
Centro Magno Guadalajara,
Comercio, Oficinas y Hotel, Guadalajara, Jal.
Plaza Marine - Novotel, Santa Fé, México D.F.
Mayan Palace – Oficinas, Guadalajara.
Mundo Mall - Oficinas, Hotel y Centro Comercial,
República Dominicana.

Corporate and Public Buildings

Centro Automotriz Del Toro, Guadalajara, Jal.
Exhibicion de Autos Washington, Guadalajara, Jal.
Fijsa Building, Guadalajara, Jal.
La Nacional Building, Guadalajara, Jal.
Chapultepec Building, Guadalajara, Jal.
Cia. Suderurgica de Guadalajara, Guadalajara, Jal.
Atemajac Market, Guadalajara, Jal.
Urban Jalisco Building, Guadalajara, Jal.
Torre Americas Building, Guadalajara, Jal.
"Miguel Hidalgo" Municipal Market, Guadalajara, Jal.
Abastos Market, extension, Guadalajara, Jal.
Droguerias Levy, Corporate Offices, Guadalajara, Jal.
Casa Jalisco, Government House, Guadalajara, Jal.
Municipal Day Nursery, Guadalajara, Jal.
Palacio Municipal Tuxtla, Chiapas.
Agencia de Autos Country Motors, Guadalajara, Jal.
Plaza Building, Guadalajara, Jal.
Conimex Building, Guadalajara, Jal.
Administrative Government Offices, Tuxtla, Chiapas.
Hewlett Packard Factory And Offices, Guadalajara, Jal.,
Projecto.
Util Building, México, D.F.
Bancomer Financial Center, Los Mochis, Sin.
Municipal Government Offices Sec. Reforma, Guadalajara, Jal.
Municipal Auditorium, Guadalajara, Jal.
Zentrum Monterrey, Monterrey, N.L.
Torre Angus Finco, Guadalajara Jal.
San Jeronimo, Corporate Offices, México, D.F.
Centro Empresarial Guadalajara, Guadalajara, Jal.
Area Comercial del Aeropuerto Miguel Hidalgo, Guadalajara.

Condominiums

Suites Andrea, Guadalajara, Jal.
El Doral, Manzanillo, Col.
Torre Country Club, Guadalajara, Jal.
Vista del Country, Guadalajara, Jal.
Cabo Real, Cabo Sn. Lucas, B.C.S.
Villas Del Tesoro, Manzanillo, Col.
Villas Gt Punta Iguana, Puerto Vallarta, Jal.
Villas Poktapok, Cancún, Q.R.
Villas Mundihotel Opequimar, Puerto Vallarta, Jal.
Suites Ritz Carlton, Cancún, Q.R.
Suites Burgos Bugambilias, Cuernavaca, Mor.
Villas Burgos Bugambilias, Cuernavaca, Mor.
Villas San Francisco Palancar, Cancún, Q.R.
Casas Villa Coral, Guadalajara, Jal.
Cabañas De Tapalpa, Tapalpa, Jal.
Isla Amorosa, Cancún, Q.R.
Isla Hechizada, Cancún, Q.R.
Isla Encantada, Cancún, Q.R.
Cabañas La Herradura, Guadalajara Jal.
Isla Magica, Cancún, Q.R.
Isla Murmullo, Cancún, Q.R.
Isla Bonita, Cancún, Q.R.
Isla Sirenas, Cancún, Q.R.

Sports Facilities

Raquet Club, Guadalajara, Jal.
Bol 2000, Guadalajara, Jal.
Santa Anita, Club House, Guadalajara, Jal.
Cumbres, Monterrey, N. L.
Universidad De Guadalajara, Guadalajara, Jal.
Social y Deportivo Jalisco, Guadalajara, Jal.
Cd. Bugambilias, Guadalajara, Jal.
Club De Tennis Isla Dorada, Cancún, Q.R.
Club Playacar, Cancún, Q.R.
Club De Playa Ixtapa, Ixtapa-Zihuatanejo, Gro.
Club De Playa Real Diamante, Acapulco, Gro.
Mexico Magico Isla Dorada

Hotels And Resorts. Selection

El Tapatio,Guadalajara, Jal.
Roma-Calinda, Guadalajara, Jal.
Plaza Las Glorias,
Puerto Vallarta, Jal
Fiesta Americana Los Angeles Locos,
Tenacatita, Jal.
Careyes, Careyes, Jal.
Fiesta Americana Rio De Janeiro, proyecto.
Fiesta Americana Vallarta, Puerto Vallarta, Jal.
Fiesta Americana Condesa, Acapulco
Fiesta Americana Cancun, Cancun, Q. R.
Continental Plaza Vallarta, Puerto Vallarta, Jal.
Villa Primavera, Guadalajara, Jal.
Plaza Las Glorias, Manzanillo, Col.
Villa Vallarta, Puerto Vallarta, Jal.
Plaza Las Glorias Puerto Iguana,
Puerto Vallarta, Jal.
John Newcombe Tennis Club,
Puerto Vallarta, Jal.
Qualton, Puerto Vallarta, Jal.
Hyatt Regency, Guadalajara, Jal.
Continental Plaza Aeropuerto, México, D.F.
Hilton Cancun, Cancún, Q.R.
Pueblo Bonito, Mazatlán, Sin.
Continental Plaza, Cancun, Q.R.
Fiesta Inn, Cancún, Q.R.
Continental Villas Plaza, Cancún, Q.R.
Continental Plaza Aeropuerto, Ii, México, D.F.
Hotel Flamingo Cancún,
Cancún, Q.R., ampliación.
Pueblo Bonito, Cabo San Lucas, B.C.S.
Plaza Las Glorias, Cozumel, Q.R.
Fiesta Inn Yukalpeten, Puerto Progreso, Yuc.
Fiesta Americana Condesa, Cancún, Q.R.
Hyatt Cancun Caribe, Cancún,
Q.R. remodelación.
Marriott Casamagna, Cancún, Q.R.
Marriott Casamagna, Puerto Vallarta, Jal.
Fiesta Americana Coral Beach, Cancún, Q.R.
Plaza Las Glorias Los Cabos,
Cabo San Lucas, B.C.S
Melia San Lucas, Cabo San Lucas, B.C.S.
Fiesta Americana Leon, León, Gto.
Plaza Las Glorias Puerto Iguana,
Puerto Vallarta, Jal.
Hilton Guadalajara, Guadalajara, Jal.
Fiesta Inn Venezuela, Higuerote, Ven.
Hyatt Regency, Mazatlán, Sin., en proceso.
Fiesta Americana Aguascalientes,
Aguascalientes, Ags.
Continental Plaza, Acapulco, Gro.
Fiesta Inn, Tepic, Nay.
Fiesta Americana Merida , Mérida, Yuc.
La Quebrada, Acapulco, Gro.
Fiesta Inn, Chihuahua, Ch.
Fiesta Inn, Monterrey, N.L.
Continental Plaza Veracruz, Veracruz, Ver.
Ritz Carlton, Cancún, Q.R.
Robinson Club Tulum, Cancún, Q.R.
Centro Vacacional Pie De La Cuesta,
Acapulco, Gro.
El Patio De Acapulco, Acapulco, Gro.
Sheraton South Padre, Padre Island, Tx.
Quinta Real, Acapulco, Gro.
Tapalpa Country Club, Tapalpa, Jal.
Sheraton, Centro Vallarta Guadalajara, Jal.
Sheraton Zentrum, Monterrey, N.L.
Hotel Piloto, Tela, Honduras.

Hotel El Presidente, Guadalajara Jal., proyecto.
Fiesta Inn, Hermosillo, Son., proyecto.
Fiesta Inn, Prototipo Motor Lobby
Holiday Inn Aeropuerto México, D.F., proyecto.
Hampton Inn, Zona Rosa México D.F.
Holiday Inn Express, Zona Rosa, México D.F.
Centro Vacacional Chapala, Chapala, Jal.
Ritz Carlton Cabo Del Sol,
Cabo San Lucas, B.C.
Fiesta Americana Caracas, Caracas, Venezuela.
Sheraton Ixtapa, Ixtapa-Zihuatanejo, Gro.
Santa Maria Del Obraje,
San Miguel Allente, Gto.
Hampton Inn Americas, Guadalajara, Jal.
Hampton Inn Tijuana, Tijuana, B. C. N.
Hampton Inn Aguascalientes,
Aguascalientes, Ags.
Hampton Inn Lomas, México D.F.
Hampton Inn Insurgentes, México, D.F.
Fiesta Americana Los Cabos.
Hotel Royal Maeva Playacar.
Hotel Playa Real, Cancún.
Hotel Amigos de la Música.
Hotel Hilton Cancún.
Hotel Grand Plaza Maya.
Hotel Arrecife Cancún.
Omni Universo, Majagua, Col.
Royal Hideaway Playacar, Q.R.
Hotel Travelodge en Lázaro Cárdenas, Mich.
The Ritz Carlton Cabos, B.C.
Hotel Casa Maya, remodelación.
Hotel Ritz Carlton Cabos.
Hotel JW Marriott, Cancún.
Hotel Fiesta Americana, Puebla.
Novotel en Plaza Marine, México D.F.
Cabo Azul Resort, Los Cabos B.C.
Royal Solaris Cabos B.C.
Royal Solaris Cancún Q.R.
Fiesta Americana Leon.
El Medano Beach Club, B.C.
Radisson Monterrey, N.L.
Secrets Punta Cana, Republica Dominicana.
Pueblo Bonito Punta Mita, Nayarit.
Ibis Guadalajara, Jalisco.
Hotel Fiesta Inn Country, Guadalajara, Jal.
Villas del Palmar, Flamingos, Nayarit.
Hotel Las Aguas, Coamo Springs, Puerto Rico.

Profile of Firm

In 1967, Jose Manuel Gomez Vazquez Aldana, a graduate architect from the University of Guadalajara, was distinguished by being awarded an Eisenhower Fellowship by the Eisenhower Exchange, allowing him among other things the chance to visit and exchange ideas with the leading architects in the United States, such as Philip Johnson, John Burgee, Morris Lapidus, Constantino Doxiadis, Walter Gropius, Mies Van Der Rohe, and I. M. Pei.

This encounter with the way United States firms work inspired him to form a world class firm in Mexico. So in 1968 the brothers Jose Manuel and Jaime Gomez Vazquez Aldana, who were already working together, joined forces and founded Gomez Vazquez Aldana & Associates, Architects and City Planners, in the city of Guadalajara.

In the beginning, the firm's area of influence was local and regional; it participated actively in tourist developments along the coast of the State of Jalisco, specially in Puerto Vallarta which was undergoing explosive growth in the late sixties and early seventies. The firm worked with the hotel industry at the time and had contacts with the leading international hotel chains, such as Hilton International, Hyatt, Sheraton, Fiesta Americana and others.

In the seventies it began a venture with the Graham-Solano interior design firm of Massachusetts, offering interior design services which led to the founding of Arquitectura de Interiores, a GVA affiliate.

Again in the seventies, work in the field of city planning and urban design represented a major portion of the firm's activities. It participated in the accelerated growth of medium-sized cities in the country, especially in the city of Guadalajara.

By the early eighties the firm's area of influence encompassed all of Mexico, working mainly on tourist and commercial developments, planning, urban design, government and administration buildings, and housing developments. At that time Architect Miguel Gomez Angulo, a member of the firm since 1968, became a partner.

In 1989 it founded a company with Peridian International of California, U.S.A., a firm in the business of landscape architecture and planning. They incorporated Peridian De Mexico so as to offer landscape architecture services.

In general the firm has grown steadily despite the continuous economic crises that have affected the world and specially this country. Thanks to diversifying the firm's fields of action and services, it has been able to adapt to market conditions and needs.

By the nineties, GVA had become one of the country's leading architecture and planning firms, participating in important projects such as the Hotel Marriott Casamagna Cancun in the Mexican Caribbean, the Hotel Marriott Casamagna Puerto Vallarta, the Hotel Ritz Carlton Cancun, the Hotel Fiesta Americana Coral Beach in Cancun, the Hotel Fiesta Americana Condesa Cancun, the Isla Dorada Residential and Nautical Development in Cancun, the Hotel JW Marriott Cancun, the Centro Magno Mall in Guadalajara, La Vista Residential Development and Golf Course in the State of Puebla, and several tourist mariners throughout the country.

In 1992, GVA entered into a strategic alliance with RTKL to take advantage of the opportunities offered by the North American Free Trade Agreement that would eventually come into effect in 1994. This strategic alliance operated efficiently and participated in different commercial and real estate developments.

Beginning in the year 2000, GVA increased its services by incorporating Idée, a graphic and environmental design company, and Casas De Mexico, a company specializing in residential designs. It also extended its sphere of influence with projects in the United States, but mainly in South America and the Caribbean.